Becky Bananas

this is your life!

Becky Bananas

this is your life!

JEAN URE

Illustrated by Mick Brownfield
and Stephen Player

Collins

An imprint of HarperCollinsPublishers

For Ann-Janine, with love and gratitude
and in the hope that we may be able to work
together again one of these days

First published in Great Britain by Collins 1997
First published in paperback by Collins 1997
This edition 2001
Collins is an imprint of HarperCollins*Publishers* Ltd
77–85 Fulham Palace Road, Hammersmith, London W6 8JB

The HarperCollins website address is: www.**fire**and**water**.com

1 3 5 7 9 8 6 4 2

Text copyright © Jean Ure 1997
Illustrations copyright © Mick Brownfield and
Stephen Player 1997

ISBN 0 00 765785 4

The author and illustrators assert the moral right
to be identified as the author and illustrators of the work.

Printed and bound in Great Britain by
Bookmarque Ltd, Croydon, Surrey

Contents

The story that follows was taken from Becky's thoughts, and hopes, and dreams as she recorded them over the last few months; also from the conversations that she had with her family and friends, and especially Sarah and Zoë.

1. "This is Your Life!"

Becky Bananas, this is your life!

Yes, it is. It is *my* life! And I have lived it for eleven and three-quarter years.

Eleven years nine months and three days, to be precise.

Eleven years nine months three days and fourteen hours, to be even more precise.

I can work it out, because I know when I was born. I was born at ten past two in the morning. Mum's told me about it heaps of times.

"You arrived all of a sudden, in this terrible rush. It took everyone by surprise, including me!"

I can never understand how it can have taken Mum by surprise. You'd think if you had a great enormous thing like a baby kicking and battering inside you, you'd feel when it was starting to come out. I should think it would be really painful.

I've asked Mum about this. She says, "It was painful, but it was worth it. Every second of it!"

But she still doesn't explain how it took her by surprise.

I said, "Didn't you feel it was happening?" and she said, "I felt *something* was happening but I wasn't quite sure what. Not until someone said 'Push!' and you came bursting out, all red and angry without any hair."

Ugh! What a yukky sight.

It seems a very odd way of carrying on if you ask me. You'd think things could have been arranged a bit better. Like with worms. Or amoebas. When amoebas want babies, they just split in half so that there are two of them.

Ever so much easier. I don't expect it hurts at all, hardly.

Not that I would want to be an amoeba. They are plain, blobby-looking creatures without any brain and they don't really seem to do anything, as far as I can see, save flop about in the bottom of pools and suchlike. But I suppose they are happy.

Can you be happy, if you haven't any brain?

At least you wouldn't be *un*happy, I shouldn't think. Or scared. Or cross or lonely or saying to yourself that things aren't fair. But then you wouldn't be able to dance or laugh or read books, either. So on the whole I wouldn't want to be one.

How could you cuddle a baby amoeba?

There are lots of pictures of Mum cuddling me. There's also a picture of me completely naked, waving my arms about on a blanket.

I've always found that really embarrassing. If I grow up and have babies, I will never take those sorts of pictures of them.

Sometimes when my friends come round, Mum pulls out the photograph albums and shows them. She says, "Look!" and she giggles. "There's Becky when she was only a few weeks old... like a little pink slug!"

Mum thinks it's funny, but I can see that other people are just as embarrassed as I am. Sarah once said, "Isn't it frightful, the way your parents come out with these terrible things?"

She meant her parents as well as Mum. Everyone's parents. *All* parents. But I don't think Mum means to say terrible things. She just can't stop herself. It's what comes of being an extrovert, which is a word I learned from Mrs

Rowe. She said it to me last Parents' Day. She said, "Your mother is quite an extrovert, Rebecca, isn't she?"

I didn't know what it meant. I asked Sarah and she said it meant that you laugh a lot and are friendly.

Deanne Warburton said it meant *noisy*.

It is true that Mum does laugh more than most people and also I suppose her voice is quite loud. But she can't help it! It's just the way she is. That's why she's in show business.

I love my mum. She is beautiful and funny and I am really proud of her. I don't mind her being loud! I wouldn't want her any different. But I do wish she wouldn't keep showing people the picture of me as a little pink slug! I won't ever do that to my children, if I have any. Which most probably I won't, I don't expect.

On the other hand, I might. You never can tell. But if I do, I won't embarrass them.

Another of the things Mum says about me is that I was a bonny bouncing baby. "Oh, you were *such* a bonny bouncing baby!"

She's got this story about how one time I bounced so high I almost managed to bounce right out of my playpen.

13

She says, "I used to think you'd end up being a pole vaulter in the Olympics!"

If ever they decide to do one of those *This is Your Life* programmes about me, like for instance when I am a famous dancer, Mum will be able to come on and tell all the people that are watching about me bouncing out of my playpen. She'd like that.

I'm not sure that I would. I think I might find it a bit embarrassing. But I suppose if you are on *This is Your Life* you can't always choose what people say about you. More's the pity!

Oh, she was such a bonny bouncing baby!

Poor Mum. Sometimes when I'm tempted to feel sorry for myself, I start thinking about Mum and feel sorry for her, instead. All that pain when I was being born, and what was the point of it? Just a waste of effort, really. That's what I would think.

I've made her cry, I know I have. I've heard her crying, when she doesn't know I was there. I can't bear for Mum to be unhappy! But when I've tried talking to her about it, like one time I said about it being a waste of effort, it made her really upset. She said, "Becky, you must never, ever think like that! What a dreadful thing to say! It was the most wonderful day of my life, the day I had you."

She didn't know how things were going to turn out. People don't, when you have babies.

Like Violet, Gran's best friend, who used to teach me dancing and who had this son called Bobby that was Down's syndrome. I remember once I was at

Gran's and Gran and Violet were talking, and Violet suddenly burst out, "I wouldn't change my Bobby for the world!"

I suppose if you have a baby, you love it no matter what. Even if it's got two heads or is brain-damaged. It's still your baby. But it would be ever so much better if things didn't happen like brain damage and Down's syndrome and such. Not till you're really old, and then perhaps it wouldn't matter quite so much. I think God should have arranged it so that everyone is allowed to live to be at least forty. I don't think you would mind so much then.

I am going to live to be a hundred. Ha! That will surprise them. Except that nobody will be here by then. Only Danny. And he will be ninety-three!!!

this is my
Little Brother

What will the date be when I am a hundred? It will be… 2086! And I will get a telegram from the Queen.

No, I won't, because the Queen won't still be alive. And I don't think Prince Charles will, either. I don't know how old he is but I think he must be older than Mum. So it won't be King Charles III. And it won't be William V, because Wills is sixteen and that would make him 103 and practically no one lives to be 103. And it won't be King Henry, I shouldn't think, because Harry would be 100 and I bet there's never been a king that's 100. But whoever it is, they will send me a telegram!

I wonder what they say when they send telegrams?

The only trouble is, you couldn't really have much fun if you were a hundred. You wouldn't be able to play games or go to parties or visit Wonderland. You'd just sit about in a chair all day wearing false teeth.

Yeeuch! I can't stand false teeth. There's this old woman I saw once that had taken hers out and put them in a glass of water by the side of her bed.

Ugh. It made me feel really sick. I don't ever want to have false teeth.

Maybe I won't live to be a hundred. Maybe I'll just live to about... forty. That's probably long enough.

I once heard Mum say to her friend Anna when they were speaking on the telephone that she was going to hold a big party when she was forty. She said it was going to be a special farewell party.

"Farewell to my lost youth... before I go into my zimmer frame."

Zimmer frames are what old people use to help them walk.

But you have to be *really* old for that. I can't imagine Mum being really old. I can't imagine her having grey hair and wrinkles.

Mum says that she can't, either, so I expect she will have a face-lift and dye her hair. That is what people in show business quite often do. They also, sometimes, have their noses altered or their boobs made bigger, to make themselves look more beautiful.

Gran used to say, "We didn't do that in my day," but Mum said, "Go on! I bet you wore falsies."

I thought she meant false teeth. It was ages before I discovered that falsies were special padded bras to make people think you had big boobs when in fact you only had small ones, though personally I can't think why anyone would want big boobs. I would think they must be quite heavy and get in the way, I mean if you're running or dancing, or anything. Surely they would wobble up and down? And if you were doing a pirouette, for instance, they would probably spin round faster than your head and unbalance you.

I wouldn't want to have big boobs. Sarah says it's men that like them and that's the reason women go and get them made huge. Just to please men.

Weird.

I bet in a hundred years' time people will be able to order bits of body from catalogues, like nowadays you can order clothes and things. They'll have these sections saying "Noses" or "Boobs" or "Ears", and all these different shapes and sizes.

All you'll have to do is pick out the ones you think will suit you and fill in an order form saying how many you want and when you want them fitted. Only by then things will be so advanced that you won't have to have an operation and be cut open, they will be able to change your shape simply by pointing some sort of ray gun at you which will make your body go like gloop.

Some people will even be able to do it for themselves, I shouldn't be surprised. They will have their own personal ray guns. They will wake up in the morning and think, "I don't like this nose. I am sick of this nose. I think

I will make a new one." Or if they are going on holiday, for instance, they will be able to use the gun for taking away all the bits of flab round their tummies so that they can wear their nice new bikinis and be attractive to men. Just zap! with the gun and all the flab will be melted.

Mum is always going on about flab. She hasn't got any, really. Not for an ordinary person. I mean, an ordinary showbiz person. I expect if she were a dancer she would have to do a bit of toning up. I fortunately do not have problems with fatness, though Mum says I have now lost too much weight and must start to put it on again. She is threatening to feed me on nothing but pasta and chips!!! I have told her I will end up like a beach ball but she says, "That will be the day."

When it is the year 2086 – when I am a hundred! If I decide to be a hundred – people I should think will be able to pump themselves up with special pumps if they are too thin. The pumps will inject calories into them, as many as they want. And if they are too fat they will take the calories out. It will be a bit like the sludge-gulping machines that go round the gutters gulping sludge.

It is interesting to speculate how people will say it when it is 2086. Will they say, twenty eighty-six? Or just eighty-six? Or will they say it in full? The year two thousand and eighty-six?

If they are American they will probably say two thousand eighty-six without the "and". I have noticed that Americans do this. They shorten things. Like they say math instead of maths and wash-up liquid instead of washing-up. I expect they do it to save time, as they are always frantically rushing everywhere and talking very fast and being busy.

The way I know about this is because of Susie Smith, at school. You'd think she was American, the way she talks, but she isn't. It's just that she lived there for a year. So now she calls her Mum "Mom" and writes these essays about her little sister wearing diapers.

Mrs Rowe says, "*Diapers*, Suzanne? What are *diapers*?" making like she doesn't understand. She's ever so English, Mrs Rowe.

She doesn't mind people speaking American when they are American, but she can't stand what she calls "apeing". But it's difficult not to pick things up. Like when me and Sarah saw this film where people kept shouting "Way to go!" and it started us off saying it, so that whenever we met we used to yell it at each other. "Way to *go*!"

We didn't know what it meant, but it sounded good.

We were only little, then; we were still nine. I always wanted to be nine. I don't know why. It used to be my favourite age. And then when I got to be it, it didn't feel all that much different from being eight, and so I decided that the next thing I wanted to be was eleven.

I never specially wanted to be ten. Perhaps it was because ten reminded me of decimals. I hate decimals. I also hate adding and subtracting and multiplying and dividing and everything that has numbers in it, including telephone numbers because I can't ever remember them.

Gran once told me that before I was born we didn't have great long telephone numbers like we have now. Instead of being 020 7373, for instance, you'd be a name, like Bluebell, maybe, or Elgar. Those are the only two that I can remember, but there were lots of them. I think Bluebell and Elgar are really pretty. Much better than boring old numbers.

Maybe that's why I didn't specially want to be ten. Or maybe it was because eleven was like a sort of goal. Like eleven was a really Great Age and if I got to be eleven I would have achieved something. Except that now I'm here it doesn't seem like very much at all.

My present ambition is to be twelve. If I get to be twelve I am going to go to Wonderland. *In America.* Mum has promised.

Mum always keeps her promises; she's really good

about that. Sarah's mum forgets. She once told Sarah she could come swimming with me and then at the last minute she said she hadn't said it and that Sarah had to go and visit her aunt and uncle instead.

Mum isn't like that. She *always* keeps her promises. So I know I shall go to Wonderland. I've got to. I want to so much!

It said in a book I read that if you want something badly enough you'll get it, but only if you keep it in front of you the whole time, like a vision, and "work steadily towards it". That is what I am doing. I am keeping Wonderland in front of me and I am working towards it.

I told this to Uncle Eddy and he squeezed my hand and said, "That's my girl! Go for it!"

I am going for it. Definitely, absolutely, and without question. I AM GOING TO WONDERLAND. And maybe Sarah could come with us. That would be fun!

It would be lovely if Zoë could come as well, but I know her Mum couldn't afford it and I don't think she'd let us pay because she's what Mum calls "proud". That means she doesn't like accepting charity, even for Zoë. But I could always get Mum to ask. It would be brilliant if Zoë could come! She would be so excited and we could keep it in front of us together. That would be like double determination, and then we would be bound to go.

If only one of them could come, it would have to be Zoë, because although Sarah is my oldest friend, and my best friend, Zoë is my *special* friend. And Sarah could go to Wonderland any time she wanted, so for her it wouldn't be such a treat.

I think it is ever so unfair that some people are rich and some people are poor. Like it is unfair that some people are born ugly and some people are born beautiful, and some are born stupid while others are born clever.

I know what Uncle Eddy would say. He would say, "That's the way the cookie crumbles, kiddo."

He is always using these quaint and colourful expressions. Sometimes I try using them in essays, but Mrs Rowe just puts big exclamation marks by them.

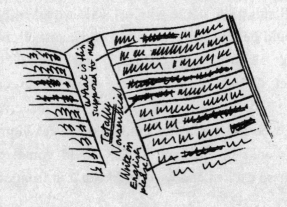

All I can say is that whoever crumbles the cookies doesn't make a very good job of it, what with big heaps here, and little heaps there, and even occasionally just crumbs.

Even sometimes nothing at all.

Being born, I must say, is a very strange and unsatisfactory experience. Why is it, for instance, that no one can ever remember it? You would think you would remember such an amazing event. For nine whole months you live in the dark, all warm and safe and tucked away, with nothing bad happening to you, and then quite suddenly you're pushed out into the world in really a very brutal rough fashion, like being squeezed headfirst out of a tube, gasping for breath and wondering whatever can be going on.

where am I?

I would think it must be quite frightening. Maybe that is why you don't remember it. Maybe it is so terrible that your brain seals it away in a little corner, never to be thought of again.

It is spooky, when you think about it. All these poor defenceless little babies being expelled from the womb with absolutely no idea what the future is going to hold. Some people, if they knew what was going to happen to them, might not want to be born at all.

If everyone was allowed to look into their future before they were born, then they could decide whether they liked it or not, and if they didn't then they wouldn't have to come, and that way perhaps there wouldn't be any more awful things such as illness and accidents and starvation.

Zoë told me that she believes everyone who dies is born again as someone else. She said, "You don't really die, because you always come back again." She told me that she read this somewhere and she most firmly believes it.

It is a nice thought but I don't understand how it can be, since the population of the world is getting bigger all the time. For example, there were probably only about – oh, I don't know! – about five hundred people, maybe, before the Stone Age, whereas now there are about five hundred million, I should think. Five hundred billion. Five hundred *trillion*. So where have all the extra people come from?

It doesn't really make any sense, though I suppose it would be a comfort to think that you weren't just going to disappear.

I asked Zoë, if you *did* come back, whether you would come as someone quite different or as just another version of yourself, and she said she'd thought about this and she reckoned you'd come back as another version of yourself. She said this would account for people sometimes claiming to remember being alive in another age.

That is true. People do make these claims. Like there was this woman who could remember being an

Egyptian slave and could even speak ancient Egyptian.

I think there may be *something* in it but that it is not quite as simple as Zoë makes out. On the other hand, if that is what she wants to believe, it would be unkind to spoil it for her by asking too many questions. We all have to find our own things to believe in. That is what Gran said and I think it is true.

What I believe is that even if I have been someone else before and am going to be someone different in the future, it is me as I am now that is important.

And me as I am now is going to go to Wonderland! That is my big, immediate goal. To be twelve years old and go to Wonderland.

I am really determined about it.

3. Me and My Favourite Things

You were born Rebecca Banaras, but everyone calls you Becky Bananas.

It was Sarah started calling me that. The first day I was at Oakfield, out in the playground at break.

"Bananas?" she said. "Is that really your name?" And before I could tell her that it wasn't, she'd gone and shrieked, "Becky Bananas!" and got everyone giggling.

I didn't think then that I was going to like her very much. But now she's my best friend and we do everything together. Well, almost everything. There are some things I can only do with Zoë, and that's why Zoë is my *special* friend. But for school and home, it's me and Sarah. We get on really well.

She'll be one of the guests when I'm on *This is Your Life*!

I don't mind her calling me Becky Bananas. I've got used to it. Once I almost wrote it on an exam paper! I got as far as:

Becky Banan

and I had to go back and change it:

Becky Bananas

We didn't have Mrs Rowe then, which is just as well or she'd have made one of her remarks like "I see we nearly stumbled at the first hurdle, Rebecca!" She said that to Sarah once, when Sarah wrote the date wrong. She can be ever so sarcastic.

And she *always* always calls us by our full names: Rebecca, Joanna, Suzanne. It's like she's scared of being too friendly. She says, "You do not shorten my name. Why should I shorten yours?"

It's hard to think how you could shorten Rowe. Sarah sometimes calls her Rosy, only not to her face. I don't think anyone would dare call her that to her face!

She's all right, really, Mrs Rowe. She's very fair. She doesn't pick on people or have favourites, like some teachers. I think she's one of those that Gran would have said their bark is worse than their bite. I wonder if she'd be one of the guests?

She might be! When I was off school last year she came to see me, which not everybody did. When I told Sarah, Sarah pulled a face and said that if she was off school a visit from Rosy was the last thing she'd want.

"Freeze the blood in your veins, that would!"

But she was really nice and not at all sarcastic. Also, she brought me a book of ballet photographs and a get-well card with a picture of Darcey Bussell on it. I wonder how she knew that Darcey is my ace favourite dancer???

Maybe she's seen the photos I've got pinned inside my locker! But she still must have gone out and bought it specially. Not everyone would have done that. So now I think that seeming to be cold and unfeeling is just her manner, like Sarah is always laughing and making jokes so that maybe you would think she doesn't care about things, but that would not be true. We wouldn't be best friends if she didn't care. For instance, she cried ever so when her favourite goldfish died.

He was called Golden Boy and it was particularly terrible and tragic as her little sister Tasha took him out of the tank when no one was looking and he squiggled through her hands and fell on the floor, and instead of putting him back she got scared and ran screaming for her mum. By the time her mum got there it was too late and he had expired (which is simply another way of saying died).

Sarah was really sad. She said that although goldfish don't have much in the way of personality it is very upsetting to think of them suffocating on the living-room carpet. I can see that it would be. Especially if it happens to be your favourite one.

We once wrote out long lists of all our favourite things, Sarah and me. We made scrapbooks and stuck them in there, with little drawings and pictures that we'd cut from magazines. Of course we were only young then. I expect if I looked at my list now I would cringe and think "How childish". I mean, for instance, when I was six years old my favourite food was – *jelly babies*!

I wonder if it would be fun to make up a new list, now that I am more mature? I think I will!

List of my Favourite Things

Favourite colour Blue. I don't know why, but it makes me happy. It is just one of those things.

Favourite book *Ballet Shoes* by Noel Streatfeild, even though it is old-fashioned. And my favourite character from *Ballet Shoes* is Posy, because she is the one who becomes a dancer!

Favourite ballet *Swan Lake*. Odette is what I want to dance more than anything else! My favourite part is where she is on point, leaning back against Prince Siegfried, and he has his arms round her.

I think that is so beautiful and romantic!

Favourite TV programme *Ask Auntie*. I have to say that because it is Mum's programme! I like it because I like to watch Mum. I suppose if Mum wasn't in it I might say… *General Practice*. I *really* like that.

Sarah says it's fuddy-duddy. That is an expression she recently read in a book and now she keeps repeating it like a parrot. Everything that she thinks dull and boring is fuddy-duddy. She says that *General Practice* is for old people. It is true that there are quite a lot of old people in it, but sometimes there are children and that is interesting. Zoë likes it, too. We have thought of writing an episode together and sending it to the BBC.

Favourite Film *Little Women*. I have seen it three times and would like to see it again, even though I always drench about ten hankies when Beth gets sick after holding poor Mrs Hummel's baby. This is because I know that she is going to die, though she doesn't actually do so in the film. (But I have read *Good Wives* and that is how I know.) Last time I watched it Mum got worried and said it was too upsetting for me. She would like it if I only watched things that made me laugh, not things that make me weep. I know she means well but you cannot cocoon people. "Wrap them in cotton wool" is what Gran used to say. I don't want to be wrapped in cotton wool. I want to watch *Little Women* again and again!

Jo of course is my favourite character. She is Sarah's too. I think she must be everyone's. The reason she is my favourite is because she is so full of life. And also because she is brave. Cutting off her hair and behaving like a boy at a time when girls were not supposed to behave like boys.

I wish I were as brave as Jo, but I don't think I am. If I were, I wouldn't choose blue as my favourite colour. I would choose... red!

I bet Jo would choose red. Red is bold and exciting. She would probably think blue is a bit boring. Uncle Eddy says it is the colour of peace and rest. That makes it sound like an old person's colour. Does it mean that *I* am like an old person?

No! It is simply that I like blue things. Blue sky. Blue sea. Blue flowers. Forget-me-nots and pansies. Harebells, bluebells. And the little trumpety things that Mum calls periwinkles.

Favourite flower My favourite of all flowers is sweet peas!

I love sweet peas because they are very dainty and fragile. Like butterflies. Gran used to grow them at the end of her garden. They grew up the fence that looked onto the railway line.

Sweet peas come in all beautiful colours. Pinks and mauves and whites and purples. Scarlets and lemons and even a sort of pale orange. But not, I think, blue. That is strange! Fancy having a favourite flower that doesn't come in my favourite colour.

When I was little I called them fairy flowers. I even made up a ballet for them.

I can't remember the steps now but I expect they were just skipping and hopping. I was only about four. I didn't know steps like *pas de chat* or *arabesque*.

Let me think of some more of my favourite things.

Favourite Animal The cat. Mum says cats are like liquid ornaments. She says she'd rather have a cat sitting on the mantelpiece than a Ming vase. I'm not quite sure what a Ming vase is, but I know that it is something very precious and expensive.

Siamese cats are *quite* expensive.

They are also very beautiful and intelligent, and also they talk all the time, in a yowling sort of way. Also, they have blue eyes!

Kitty had green ones. She was just an ordinary cat. Not like Bella and Bimbo. They are pedigrees. But she slept on my bed and she cuddled and purred. She was my very favourite cat of all.

I shall never forget Kitty.

I am still thinking of favourite things.

Favourite activity Dancing! When I was young we were too poor for me to go to a proper dancing school and so Gran's friend Violet taught me. Gran called her Vi but I called her Violet. Even when I was six years old, that is what I called her. She used to say, "I don't hold with all this formality, ducks."

Violet was younger than Gran but they'd been on tour together in the old days, when Violet was a dancer and Gran was part of a double act with Granddad. And then Violet had Bobby, who was Down's syndrome, and gave it all up to look after him. Only she would never say that she had given it up. She would say, "Gave it up? I didn't give *it* up, it gave me up!" And then she'd laugh this funny, crackling laugh and light another fag. She always called them her fags.

"Where are me fags? Pass me me fags!"

She used to smoke her fags even while she was teaching me.

I don't suppose, really, that Violet was ever a very good dancer. She never did proper ballet. I think what she did was called show dancing. But she taught me how to do *pliés* and positions of the feet, and *battements tendus* and *ronds de jambes*.

Later, when I went to the Russell, Miss Runcie said I'd had a good grounding, so Violet must have known what she was doing even if she did pronounce *ronds de jambes* as "rondy jombs".

I didn't know what Miss Runcie was talking about the first time she told us to do them. I said, "Oh, rondy jombs!" and everyone laughed and I couldn't understand why.

And then I realised and I went home and pretended to be Violet saying things wrong – rondy jombs and arabeskys and grond jetties – and Mum overheard me and told me off. She said, "Don't you *ever* let me catch you making fun of Violet again!"

Mum said that Violet was a good and genuine person who had had a great deal to cope with in life. So then I felt ashamed and regretted that I had mocked her. I wish I could tell Violet how sorry I am!

Maybe she will be one of my guests.

Then I will be able to tell her.

What are some more of my favourite things?

Favourite dancer Darcey Bussell! One Christmas Mum took me backstage to meet Darcey and she is really nice and friendly. She gave me a signed photograph and encouraged me to keep up with my dancing. She said that maybe one day it would be her coming backstage to see me!

I'd *really* want Darcey to be on the programme. If I was going to be anyone other than who I am then I would choose to be Darcey. She is everything that I dream of being.

What else is there?

Favourite season of the year
Summer.

Favourite sort of weather Sun! It is very sad and depressing, I think, in the winter, though Sarah doesn't agree. Sarah's favourite weather is snow! But that is because she likes to go skiing.

Favourite Food Just at the moment it is difficult to say as I am not terribly into food owing to my mouth being sore, but as a rule I would say it is... chocolate ice cream!

Favourite drink Pineapple milkshake. For sure!

Favourite place Covent Garden.

Favourite music *Swan Lake*! Because every time I hear it I can imagine that I am on stage, dancing!

Favourite group The Beatles. Me and Sarah are really into the Beatles. It was Mum who got us listening to them. John Lennon was her favourite Beatle. She says she cried when he got shot. My favourite is Paul. He is Sarah's, too. Imagine if he was a guest!

I think Paul is the *best* Beatle. He cares about animals, and I approve of that. I am going to stop eating animals as soon as I can. I wanted to do it when I was eleven but Mum wouldn't let me. She said it wasn't the time. Now she says, "Maybe in a year or two. We'll see."

I think I will ask her if I can do it when I'm twelve. I am going to do all sorts of things when I am twelve! Going to Wonderland is just one of them. Being twelve is my immediate goal. It is Zoë's, as well. But I will be twelve before she is! I will be twelve on 14th September. Zoë has to wait until the end of the year.

Sarah will be twelve before either of us as her birthday is next month. But to her it isn't anything particularly special. She just wants to go out with her Mum and buy a whole load of new clothes, and she could do that any time. Sarah's Mum is always buying her clothes. And she always gives her a good birthday party, too. One time she hired a bouncy castle and another time there was a conjuror. But Sarah says she wants to be more sophisticated now that she's going to be twelve.

I don't know whether I will have a party or not. I didn't last year. Not a proper one. Mum said it would be "too much". And this year I shall be in Wonderland!!! It might be greedy to ask for a party as well.

I have just thought of another favourite thing to add to my list.

Favourite person Uncle Eddy! After Mum and Danny, of course. Uncle Eddy will *definitely* be on my television programme.

Here's looking at you, kid!

Uncle Eddy is Mum's brother. She calls him her *baby* brother because she was seven when he was born. That is exactly the same difference as between Danny and me!

Of course Danny is only actually my half-brother. This is because we had different dads. I told him this once, when I was in a really mean mood. I said, "You're only my half-brother! And that's as much as I want you to be!"

I only said it because I was feeling cross and self-pitying. It wasn't anything Danny had done. I told Uncle Eddy afterwards and he said that sometimes when we're feeling hurt we take it out on other people, just because they happen to be there. He said it's a bit like getting in the way if someone's running down the street. They don't necessarily *mean* to knock you over, but that's what happens.

I didn't mean to be horrid to Danny. I wish I hadn't been. He's only a little boy! He doesn't understand.

He clambered on to my bed the other day and put his arms round my neck and whispered, "I want to be your real *whole* brother, Becky." It made me cry, that did.

Danny is a truly sensitive little boy. I think he picks up on a whole lot more than people realise, even though he is only four years old. Uncle Eddy agrees with me.

We talk a lot together, me and Uncle Eddy. The reason I love him so much is that he is like an uncle and a dad and a big brother and a best friend, all rolled into one. He is also, quite simply, the most beautiful person I have ever seen. The most beautiful man, that is. (Darcey is the most beautiful woman. After Mum!)

Zoë agrees with me about Uncle Eddy. She says that her insides go "all tingly" just at the sight of him. Even Sarah admits that he is quite hunky, and Sarah is a very difficult person to impress.

But I would love him just as much if he had cross eyes and a hump back and horrible whiskers growing out of his nose! (Which is what some men have and which really puts me off.)

I wouldn't care what he looked like, he would still be my favourite person. After Mum and Danny.

One way I am lucky is that Uncle Eddy isn't married and therefore has no children of his own. If he had children of his own I wouldn't see him nearly as often, because why would he leave them to come and see boring old me? It wouldn't be fair.

I am glad he isn't married! I expect that is selfish, but I don't care. I don't want him ever to be!

Well, not for a *long* time in case his wife got cross and said, "Oh, you are surely not going off to visit that stupid, dim child again? I want you to spend more time with me!"

Sometimes people's wives are like that. Like Zoë's dad's wife. Zoë's dad got married again after he and Zoë's mum were divorced and now he lives in Yorkshire and Zoë hardly ever see him. Even once when she was really sick and her mum called him and he came down, he could only stay one night because of his wife.

"She can't manage on her own." That's what he said. So he went back off to Yorkshire and I don't know when was the last time that Zoë saw him. I feel really sorry for her. That's why I let her share Uncle Eddy. I wouldn't let just anyone. Mostly I would like to keep him all to myself.

If Uncle Eddy got married and had children I would probably be jealous of them. That is another reason I don't

52

want him to do it. And maybe he won't because me and Sarah have discussed it and we think that perhaps he is gay. Elinor Hodges, at school, says we didn't ought to talk about things like that. Not at our age. But I don't see why we shouldn't, there's nothing wrong with it. Being gay, I mean. Mum has lots of friends who are.

I expect she'd tell me if I asked her, she's always told me everything, like about babies and everything, long before we did it at school, but I'm scared to ask in case she laughs and says "No! What on earth made you think that?" She might tell me that Uncle Eddy has a million beautiful girlfriends, scattered all over the globe, and then my dream would be shattered.

My dream is that when I grow up he will ask me if I would like to go and live with him in a flat overlooking Hyde Park. Of course I know it is not very likely to happen, but that is my secret dream.

What Uncle Eddy does is, he makes me feel brave. I think I am quite wimpish, actually. Not like Zoë. She is brave. I can't imagine Zoë ever being scared of anything.

Or Sarah, although Sarah as far as I know does not have anything to be scared of. She is lucky. Some people just are.

It is when I am on my own sometimes that I get frightened. I have these thoughts, and they scare me. But when Uncle Eddy is here, I feel like – like I could do anything! Like there is absolutely no reason to be frightened. Because while he is here you just know that nothing bad could ever happen. He is that sort of person.

They are my golden days, when Uncle Eddy is here. He comes whenever he can but quite often he is away on location. Being a TV cameraman means that he has to go all over the world, like at the moment he is in Africa.

I wish he was here! But I know that he can't be. When you are away filming you cannot simply drop everything and come running back home. It is not like an ordinary job where you can just say to your secretary, "Tell them that I am out of the office" or "I will deal with it later". If Uncle Eddy is not there, then there is nobody to work the camera and the programme cannot be made.

It is no good wishing that I could have golden days all the time. I am lucky to have any at all. I know this.

I probably shouldn't have thought of Uncle Eddy. It is silly thinking of things that upset you.

I will think of some more favourites.

No, I won't! I will think about when I was little.

5. Bow Bells

*You were born in London, within the sound
of Bow bells.*

I am a true Cockney! Like Gran. The only way you can call yourself a Cockney is if you are born within the sound of the Bow bells.

Mum always tells people that she is one, but she isn't because she wasn't born there. She was born in Manchester, when Gran and Granddad were on tour. And Uncle Eddy was born on the Isle of Wight. I am the only one – apart from Gran – who is a real, true, actual Cockney!

I said this to Mum once and she laughed and told me not to be so pedantic. When I asked her what pedantic meant she said, "Boringly sticking to the absolute truth." Well! I thought that was what you were supposed to do. But Mum insists that "For all intents and purposes I am a Cockney", and that is what she tells people when they come to interview her for magazines, etc.

Uncle Eddy is more Cockney than Mum because he didn't go to drama school and get rid of his accent. He still talks what Mum calls "gorblimey". She is always mimicking him, and pulling his leg, but Uncle Eddy doesn't mind. I wish I could talk Cockney like he does! I probably would have done if Mum had let me, but she always used to keep on about how I had to speak properly.

I don't see that speaking like Mum does, is any more proper than the way Uncle Eddy speaks. Uncle Eddy thinks it's a joke.

"Gotta talk nice," he says; and then he winks at me behind Mum's back.

Uncle Eddy calls me his little Cockney sparrow (only the way he says it, it sounds more like "me liddle Cockney sparrer") and he's taught me all this rhyming slang. Sarah and me sometimes use it when we want to mystify people. Like Sarah might say, "I'll be on the dog, Saturday morning," and I'll know she's going to ring me. Or I might tell her that Mum's meeting me after school to go and buy me some Daisy Roots, and everyone will look at me as if I've gone mad, but Sarah will nod and say, "Doc Marten's?"

Oh, and one time when Mrs Rowe was collecting money for something, Sarah couldn't find her purse and she cried, "Some rotten tea leaf has gone and nicked it! All my bread has gone!"

It was really funny because Mrs Rowe didn't have the faintest idea what she was talking about. She doesn't understand *any* Cockney slang.

Once when we walked into the classroom there was this simply terrific stink coming from outside, and Sarah said, "Cor, wot a pen!" and Mrs Rowe said, "Please don't use expressions like that, Sarah. It's not very becoming." And Sarah said, "But there is a pen! It's horrible!" and Mrs Rowe looked all round and said, "Indeed? Point it out to me. I observe no pens of any description."

She thought Sarah was talking about fountain pens!

This is some of the Cockney slang that Uncle Eddy has taught me:

Pen and ink

Titfer tat

Daisy Roots

Currant bun

Bread and honey

Hampstead Heath

Jam jar

Mince pies

Boat race

North and south

Apples and pears

Mutt and Jeff

Dog and bone

Plates of meat

Rosie Lee

Tea leaf

When I was little and Gran used to talk about having a nice cup of Rosie, I never knew why she called it that. Like with titfer. She would say, "Nasty cold wind out there. Not going out without me titfer." So I always knew that Rosie was tea and titfer was hat, but it wasn't until Uncle Eddy explained that it was rhyming slang that I really understood.

There is another one he told me which is a naughty one. When Uncle Eddy needs to go to the toilet he says, "I gotta have a gypsy's." That is short for "gypsy's fiddle" and it means… piddle! I would love to say that to Mrs Rowe!!!

I wish I were bold enough. I don't have any bottle at all. But Sarah does! I think I shall suggest it to her. If I dared her, she would do it.

Bottle is also Cockney slang. It is short for bottle and glass. I don't know what it is supposed to rhyme with but when Uncle Eddy says that someone has no bottle he doesn't mean what I used to think he meant when I was small.

man with bottle

man without bottle

He means that they're not very brave. Like me. I hate myself sometimes for being so bottle-less. Like when I have to have injections and I cry. That is an example of not having any bottle.

Uncle Eddy says that he is scared of injections. He quite often has to have them when he goes abroad. He says, "They frighten the living daylights out of me!" But I think he is only saying it to be kind. I am such a crybaby!

I haven't always been. I remember Gran had to take me to the hospital once because I fell off my bike and cut my hand and had to have stitches, and all the time they were stitching me I just, like, ground my teeth and never made a sound. Gran was ever so proud of me! She said I was brave as ninepence (ninepence is to do with olden-times money) and that I deserved to have a special treat and "something nice for tea" so she bought this beautiful pink cake with pink icing and we ate it in the kitchen with Violet and Bobby.

I'll always remember Gran's cake with pink icing. Cakes with pink icing mean you have bottle. I wouldn't have any cakes with pink icing now. And I don't think Gran would call me brave as ninepence. Gran would be *ashamed* of me.

Gran had a really hard life. I know this because

Mum told me so. But Gran faced up to things. She wouldn't have cried just because people kept sticking needles in her. And I bet Uncle Eddy doesn't, either. He's not really frightened of injections. Uncle Eddy isn't frightened of anything! He just says it to make me feel better. And to try and make me be brave.

But I can't be brave! I've tried and tried and I can't. I hate it! My body is getting to be like a pincushion, all sore and covered in holes. If they keep on like this, my blood will start leaking!

I don't want to think about things like that.

I'm not going to think about things like that! I'm only going to think about things that make me happy.

6. My Gran

For the first few years of your life you lived in Samuel Street, in Bethnal Green.

We lived with my Gran and Uncle Eddy in Gran's house where Mum and Uncle Eddy were brought up. The house was very little and old. It was squashed in the middle of a row of other little, old houses, all the same.

Downstairs there was a front room and a back room and a kitchen. Mum used to complain that it was dark and poky. Some people in the street had knocked down the wall between the front room and the back room to make one large room. Mum wanted Gran to do it in her house, but Gran wouldn't. She said, "Lose all me privacy that way."

She had a piano in the front room which she called "a Joanna". I don't know why she called it that. Maybe Joanna is also Cockney slang. If you called a piano a pianner then it would rhyme, so maybe that is it.

Gran said that the Joanna was mine and I could play on it, but I wasn't ever very good.

Later I went to Mrs Dearborn and did it properly, scales and things, but Mrs Dearborn said that although I was musical I would never make a pianist. But that was all right because I didn't want to be a pianist, I wanted to be a dancer. Ever since I was tiny I have wanted to be a dancer. Being twelve is my *immediate* goal, but being a dancer is my Big Ambition.

Sometimes people expect me to want to be an actress, because of Mum, but I don't think I would like that. For one thing I wouldn't like having to learn lines. Learning steps is different: you learn with your feet. When I have done a step once, I can remember it. With lines you have to go over and over them. Mum is always grumbling about it.

And then for another thing there is *resting*, which

means being out of work sometimes for months or even years. I think with dancing that wouldn't happen so much because if you were in a dance company you would be dancing all the time.

Of course I realise you might not be lucky enough to get into a dance company and then you would have to do something ordinary, like working in a shop or being a waitress, but that is what Mum would call "thinking negatively". Thinking negatively is a bad thing to do. So I am not going to do it. I am only going to think positive things, such as going to Wonderland.

Remembering is a positive thing. Mum couldn't say that was negative. She is always taking out the photograph albums and all her press cuttings. That is what I am doing, except that I am doing it in my mind. I am remembering Gran's house.

Upstairs there were three bedrooms and a teeny tiny

bathroom without any toilet. The toilet was downstairs in the yard. It was spooky going out there at night so when I was little I used to have something that Gran called a jerry, but which most people call a potty.

I asked Gran once why she called it a jerry and she said because that was what *her* gran had called it, but then she stopped to think and she said it was probably because in the First World War people had referred to the Germans as "Jerries" and the German helmets had looked a bit like potties.

So now that is what I always call them. If I ever have a baby I will not put her on the potty, I will put her on the jerry. I think that potty is a silly and childish word. All it means is a little pot. It is baby talk!

Another word Gran used to use for it was "po", which I thought was rude until Mum explained that it was simply the French word for pot. The French pronounce pot as po! But I still think that po sounds vulgar.

It is strange how many different expressions there are for such a small and insignificant object.

Like all those words for lavatory. There is Ladies & Gents, with the little signs.

There is WC (which stands for water closet).

There is bog (which Uncle Eddy sometimes says).

There is karzy (which he also sometimes says and which I don't know how to spell).

There is loo, though this is really just the French word for water. *L'eau*. Loo is how it got to be said in this country. In Edinburgh, in the olden days, when people used to empty their chamber pots out of their bedroom windows, they used to shout "Gardy loo!" to warn the passers-by.

They really meant "*Gardez l'eau*". Watch out for the water! Mademoiselle LeClerq told us this at school.

Gran's toilet got a bit pongy sometimes, because of the damp and being outside. Also, it used to have spiders in there.

All the rooms in Gran's house were absolutely tiny, even the big back bedroom where Mum and me slept. Uncle Eddy used to sleep at the front and Gran had the littlest one of all. Gran's bedroom was like a cupboard but Gran said that she was old and didn't need much space.

"Not like a growing lad."

That was Uncle Eddy! It is odd to think that when I was born he was only –

I am not very good at sums. Mum is thirty-three. And I am eleven. That means that when I was born Mum was twenty-two. And Uncle Eddy is seven years younger than Mum, so he was...

Fifteen! I can hardly believe it. That is the same age as Sarah's brother.

I loved it at Gran's. Outside in the yard she had a row of giant toadstools that Granddad had made for her. I think they were made from cement. Or stone, or something. They were painted bright red with big white spots and I used to spend hours trying to jump from one to another without falling off.

Kitty used to jump with me.

At night when I went to bed she would come and sleep with me, all curled up on the pillow, right next to my head.

When the trains went past you could see the lights from the carriages flickering on the wall. I asked Mum where the trains were going and she said they were going to Stratford and Bow. I thought it sounded incredibly romantic. I was only very little, then. I didn't realise that Stratford and Bow were just up the road.

There was a sweet shop on the corner of Samuel Street. It was owned by a lady called Mrs Platt who had a big bosom. Once I went in there with Stacy Kitchin who lived next door and we stole things. I stole a bar of chocolate and Stacey stole a packet of crisps. We did it while Mrs Platt was serving someone. She never knew.

I don't think she did. She never said anything about it. But quite soon after that she put up this notice saying, "Only two school children in the shop at any one time", so maybe she did after all.

I feel really bad about it now.

Mrs Platt is someone else it would be nice if I could say sorry to.

I don't know why we stole things. I suppose we thought it would be exciting. It must have been Stacey's idea; she was always the one that had the ideas. I just followed. Mum never liked me playing with Stacey. She said she was a bad influence. She never liked having to live with Gran, either. She loved Gran, but she didn't like having to live with her.

It was because we didn't have enough money to buy a home of our own. Mum didn't work very much in those days. Not on television. Sometimes in the theatre, and sometimes she had to go away on tour and then she used to leave me with Gran. I didn't mind. I loved being with Gran! Mum said she spoilt me, but she didn't. She was quite strict. For example, she wouldn't ever let me use bad language or stay out late.

We used to play in the street, me and Stacey and some other kids that lived on the block. Once when Gran came to call me in I ran off and hid and she got really mad. She stood on the front doorstep and yelled, "Becky Banaras! You come here this instant or I'll tan your hide!"

I think to tan your hide means to wallop someone, but Gran never did that. She just used to slap my legs and tell me I was a "little bleeder".

When I am on *This is Your Life* it will be too late for Gran. But I will think about her! She said to me before she died, "When you have loved someone, they are with you always." And I do believe this to be true because sometimes I can feel Gran with me even now.

I hear her saying things to me, such as, "You just pull your finger out, my girl!" if I'm being lazy, for example. Or if I wake up in the night feeling a bit wimpish and scared she'll whisper, "Don't you worry, my lovey! You hang on in there. It'll all come right in the end." And that makes me feel stronger and gives me some bottle.

It is strange to reflect that if I had had a dad the same as other people, I might never have gone to live with Gran. I loved my Gran so much! I wish she hadn't died. I know that everybody has to, sooner or later, but when it happens it is so sad to know that you can never see the person again. Not until you die yourself, and then you will meet in the afterlife and it will be as if no time at all has passed, as if it was just yesterday.

This at least is what I believe.

7. Reflections

*Your parents got married when they were students,
but you never met your dad.*

I've never even met him. My own dad! He and Mum stopped being in love with each other before I was born. I think that is so sad, when people stop being in love with each other. Gran used to say, "I warned them, but they wouldn't listen."

The problem was that they got married when they were too young. That is what Gran used to say. They were students together at drama school and they were only nineteen. But Mum says she doesn't regret a moment of it. She says that it was wonderful while it lasted. She says that young love is the most passionate and the most romantic kind that there is. I wonder if I shall ever experience it???

Another thing Mum says, and she always smiles sort of sloppily as she says it, is that "Hari was very good-looking."

Hari was my dad. He was Indian. He came from Madras, which I have often looked at on the map.

Just in case one day I might bump into him in the street and not know who he was, though unfortunately I don't think this is very likely as he went back home to India and Mum thinks this is where he probably stayed. She says his mum and dad didn't like it when he came to England to be a drama student. Also they didn't like it when he married Mum. It wasn't because they didn't like English people, just that they would have liked it better if he had married an Indian lady.

I expect by now he probably has. I think she will be very beautiful and have a red spot in the middle of her forehead and wear a sari and that they will have four children.

I wish I could have met him just once! How lovely it would be if he woke up one day and said, "I think I will go and visit my daughter in England." And then he would turn up, all handsome, on the doorstep, and people would wonder, "Who is that gorgeous man?" and will not realise he is my dad!

Maybe when I am on television they will be able to find him and he will fly over specially to appear on the programme!

The name Banaras is a particularly special sort of name as it is another way of spelling Benares, which is the Holy City of the Hindus. Mum suggested once that I might like to change my name to something more English so that people wouldn't call me Bananas all the time. She said, "You could change to Danny's name, if you wanted." But Danny's name is Martin, and Martin is an *ordinary* name.

I like being called after a holy city! And Mum never changed her name. At least, she did for when she has to sign cheques or anything official. Then she's Marianne Martin. But when she's on TV or being interviewed she's Marianne Jacobs, the same as she always was. So I am going to stay as I am!

Violet used to have this dog that was a cross between a German sausage and a Yorkshire terrier.

I am a cross between Indian and English.

I am also a cross between Hindu and Jewish. My dad was Hindu and my mum is Jewish. I think that is interesting. The Hindu religion is very colourful, it has Lord Krishna and lots of gods with names such as Siva and Vishnu. It also has Diwali, which is the Festival of Lights. You can buy nice cards at Diwali and send them to your Hindu friends if you have any.

If I knew where my dad lived, I could send one to him. I would write in it, "Happy Diwali! With love from your daughter in England." And I would put my address in case he decided to come and see me.

The Jewish religion is in the Old Testament. It is full of ancient history and exciting stories, like the one about David and Goliath. It also has festivals. My favourite is Hanukkah because you get presents!

I could be whichever religion I choose. I could be Hindu or I could be Jewish. At the moment I am not either. Maybe I won't ever be. Maybe I'll just be me.

I'm not too sure about religion. God, and everything.

I expect there might be a god of some sort, because otherwise how did we get here? But I don't see how anybody can know. Not for certain. It seems a bit odd to me, going and worshipping someone that might not exist. And even if he did – though it might be a she – how do we know that it wants us to worship it, necessarily? And *why* would it want us to worship it?

I tried talking to Mrs Rowe about this, but she wasn't very helpful. She said, "Surely we are worshipping God in order to give thanks for our existence?"

I said, "But suppose it's a miserable existence like it is for people that are starving or paralysed after motor accidents?"

All she did was lift her shoulders and say, "We must all take our chance in this world."

Another time she told me that "You have some very strange ideas, Rebecca."

I don't see what's strange about my ideas. Neither does Uncle Eddy. When I talked to him about God he said he didn't think that a god that was worth worshipping would actually *want* to be worshipped. So then I asked him if he thought it was all right not to be religious but just to be yourself, and he said he didn't see why not. He said that some people feel the need for religion, and some don't. There are some people, for example, where religion gives meaning to their lives. (But my life already has meaning! I am going to be a dancer.) Then there are other people that religion is a comfort to, when they are ill, for instance, or afraid of dying.

I have done a lot of thinking about this. I have tried very hard to believe in God, because I think it would be nice and that it *would* be a comfort. But I can't. So I think I might as well give up trying.

What I believe is what Gran said. When Gran knew she was going to die she told me that it wasn't anything to be scared of. She said that when you were dead you got to meet up with all the people that had gone before you.

I said, "In heaven?" and she said, "You can call it heaven, if you like. It's only another name for what lies beyond."

Gran said she was looking forward to it. She was sorry she would have to say goodbye to me and Danny, and Mum and Uncle Eddy, but she knew she'd see us all again one day. She said, "In the meantime, darling, we must be patient." She said, "I've lived a long time and I'm tired." She said that life beyond was going to be lovely and peaceful "after all this strife". No more pain or misery. No more wars or cruelty or people starving.

I said that it sounded beautiful, but it made me so sad to think that Gran wouldn't be here any more. That was when she told me that if you've loved someone, they would be with you always. She said, "You might not be able to see me, but I'll be around. Never fear!" And she is, I know that she is.

She told me that she was really disappointed that she wouldn't get to see me grow up and become a famous dancer, but on the other hand she couldn't wait to be with Granddad again. So although I missed her terribly, I knew that she was happy and that it would be selfish to want her back.

Mum agreed. She said, "Your gran was in a lot of pain at the end. It was a blessing for her when she went."

I hadn't been thinking about the pain; I'd just been thinking of her being with Granddad. Gran loved Granddad ever so much. She kept a big photograph of him on her bedside table and she told me that she never went to sleep without saying goodnight to him, even though he'd been dead for years and years.

Granddad died before I was born. And I've never seen my Indian grandparents, so Gran was the only one I ever had. Sarah has *four*.

I've met one of Sarah's grans. She isn't like a gran at all. She wears these really trendy clothes, including short skirts that show all her legs.

And her eyes are all spikey with mascara, and she has these incredibly long nails, like claws, that she paints blood red.

I'm glad my gran wasn't like that!

My gran was a real gran. She was little and old and she had white hair.

I think this is how a gran should be. A gran shouldn't be glamorous, she should be soft and cuddly and comfortable. My gran was all of those things. I know she sometimes smacked my legs when I was naughty, but she always came and tucked me up at night and once when I had a really bad dream and Mum was away she let me go and sleep with her in her big old bed where she had slept with Granddad. I can't imagine Sarah's gran letting her do that.

Gran's bed was so big it took up almost the whole of her bedroom but she wouldn't ever get rid of it because of her memories of Granddad. That is how much she loved him.

My gran was born in Bethnal Green, just two streets away from Samuel Street. She lived there the whole of her life (except when she and Granddad were on tour). She spoke Cockney even better than Uncle Eddy does. Mum used to shake her head and say, "Honestly, Ma! I couldn't take you anywhere." She used to call her a denizen: Denizen Daise, on account of her name being Daisy.

I didn't know what a denizen was so I asked Violet and she said it was "sort of like an inhabitant... someone that lives somewhere."

It didn't make any sense to me. Why should Mum call Gran a person that lived somewhere?

Next time she said it, I asked her. I said, "Why are you calling Gran a person that lives somewhere?" and she said, "I'm not. I'm calling her a denizen," and I said, "Denizen means someone who lives somewhere," and Mum said, "Not when I use it. When I use it, it means low life." And she laughed as she said it.

Gran laughed, too, as if she didn't in the least bit mind being called low life, so that now I think perhaps it must have been some kind of joke between them.

Sometimes when Mum and Eddy talk about Gran, Mum still refers to her as "the poor old denizen", though not at all in a nasty way. I think she really loved her.

I like to hear Mum and Uncle Eddy remembering the old days, when they were young. Uncle Eddy says that Mum was the bane of Gran's life.

"A proper little madam!"

She was always getting into trouble, my mum. Uncle Eddy told me that one time when she'd given

Gran some really bad mouth and Gran had lost her temper, Mum had come galloping out of the kitchen and up the stairs with Gran chasing behind her "yelling blue murder and taking these swipes with a tea towel".

Eddy   marianne

He said that Mum got to the top of the stairs, shouted "Ha ha! Missed me!" and dived into her bedroom before Gran could get her.

That sounds like Mum! She always has an answer for everything. "Smart mouth," Uncle Eddy says.

I wish I were a smart mouth! I would love to be able to think of clever things to say. But I can't, and even if I could I would be too afraid of getting into trouble. I hate it when people are cross. Mum just doesn't seem to care.

I don't think I take after Mum very much at all. I think I probably take after my dad, though of course it is hard to tell when I have never met him.

There can't be many people that have never met their dads. I should think it is quite unusual. You would have thought he would at least have stayed to see what I looked like, but Mum says he didn't want them to have a baby because a) he didn't think they could afford one and b) he was scared it might interfere with his career as an actor.

It is hard not to have feelings of rejection, knowing that your own dad didn't want you. Mostly I try not to think about it but just now and again it comes back to me and I get a little sad. Mum says she ought not to have told me and that she can't imagine why she did. She says, "My wretched tongue runs away with me! I always was a blabbermouth. You ask your Uncle Eddy… he'll tell you!"

But I expect it is only right that I should know about such things. I can understand my dad thinking they could not afford me as I am sure a baby is quite an expensive thing to run, what with nappies and prams and suchlike. It would have been nice, all the same, to have known him.

8. My Brother Danny

When you were seven years old, your brother
Danny was born.

I was really jealous of Danny when he was born. I didn't think it was fair that he should have a dad and I didn't, especially as he'd sort of, in a way, Danny's dad I mean, been my dad before Mum went and had Danny.

I'm sorry now that I was jealous. It wasn't Danny's fault. He couldn't help it. And he's never minded me sharing. Even after I was mean to him that time and told him he was only my half-brother, he still talked about "Daddy" as if he belonged to both of us. If he'd wanted to be mean back to me he could have started calling him "*My* daddy". But Danny isn't like that. He is a truly nice little boy. He's ever so quiet and gentle. Not like some of them that run around shouting and fighting all the time.

I wish I'd played with him more! His most favourite game of all is having a teddy bears' picnic with his soft toys. Danny has loads of soft toys. There's Bruin the

Bear and Winnie the Wallaby and a dirty old pink rabbit called Clyde that he used to suck when he was a baby. Then there's Roly Rat and Dolly the Donkey and Horace, the hand-knitted giraffe. And of course there's Teddy, who used to be Mum's and then was Uncle Eddy's and then was mine and now belongs to Danny. Teddy's been mended heaps of times. He's really old and moth-eaten, but if ever you ask Danny which one he likes best he always says "Teddy!"

I should have played with him. He loves it when I join in. I give all the animals different voices, like high and s-q-u-e-a-k-y for Roly Rat and dark and DEEP for Bruin the Bear. And "Ee-aw ee-aw!" for Dolly the Donkey. And "Bloop bloop" for Winnie and "Woffle woffle" for Clyde. Danny gets all giggly and bunches his hands into little fists and stuffs them in his mouth. He's so funny!

Mum took us to a special children's show last Christmas and afterwards she asked us if we'd enjoyed it and which our favourite bits were. Danny said, "I liked the bit where the man fell over." Mum said, "But that was an accident! The poor man caught his foot in something. It wasn't meant to happen!" Danny said, "That was the *funniest* bit. I liked that bit." And he chuckled away ever so happily. Mum shook her head and said, "I don't know!" But he's only four years old. Four is very young.

That's why I wish I'd been nicer to him and made more time for him. I wonder if everyone looks back on their life and has regrets or if it's only me?

When Danny comes on my programme I'll make it up to him! I'll give him an enormous great kiss and tell everyone that's watching that he is my real, *whole* brother. I will, I promise!

Danny's dad is called Alan Martin. He's quite a nice person, really. I wouldn't have minded if he'd stayed married to Mum. Mum brought him to our Open Day once and everyone went "Ooh" and "Aah" because they'd seen him acting with her on television.

He's in America now, making movies. Maybe when I'm on *This is Your Life* they could do a satellite link-up so that he could say "Hi!" They do that, sometimes, when people are living in another country and don't want to make long journeys.

I don't think he'd fly over specially. I shouldn't think he would. Not just for me. He sends me a present at Christmas and on my birthday, the same as he does Danny, but we don't ever see him. He's married to an American lady and they have a baby of their own called Emerald.

I think it must be sad for Danny, knowing his dad has another baby that he loves more than he loves him. If he didn't love her more, he'd come to England and visit us. He does speak sometimes on the phone, but it isn't the same. Sometimes the line is crackly and once we heard Emerald bawling in the background. And Danny is always tongue-tied and never knows what to say.

Maybe Mum will get married again. Actresses often do.

It was ever so posh, when she got married to Alan. "A really glitzy do" is what Uncle Eddy called it. Not like when Mum married my dad, when they didn't have any money and just went up the road to the local registry office.

Mum and Alan also got married in a registry office, because of both of them having been married before and not being allowed to do it in church, but their registry office was a smart one, in Kensington. We all got dressed up in our best clothes. I had a special new dress made, orange and rose-pink, with a bunch of flowers to carry and confetti to throw. And loads of photographers came to take photographs for the papers because now that Mum was in *Ask Auntie* she was famous.

It was very strange at first, Mum being famous. It meant that everyone knew who she was and recognised her in the street so we couldn't go anywhere without people coming up and asking her for her autograph.

Sometimes it was really funny, like when we were

shopping in Safeway and this woman came rushing across the store and peered up at Mum and shouted, "It's her! It is!" and this other woman that had been waiting immediately came flying over and asked Mum if she'd mind her looking in our trolley. She said, "I like to know what the stars are buying."

Mum and I giggled over that. For ages afterwards, whenever any of her friends came round, Mum used to act it out for them. She'd make me be her, pushing the trolley, and she'd be the two women. Everyone always went into shrieks of laughter.

But later on, when Mum and Alan decided they didn't love each other any more, it was horrible. There were all these headlines in the papers.

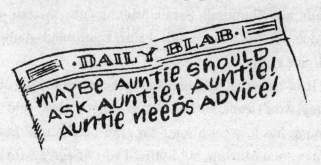

And then underneath they went on about how Mum and Alan weren't going to live together any more. They seemed to think it was amusing. Just because Mum played the part of an agony aunt on the telly.

I can see now why they call them agony aunts. When people write them letters all about their problems, I expect they probably are in agony. Especially if they are quite well known and everyone recognises them and they are being written about in the newspapers. It isn't very nice having to go into school and knowing that everyone knows all about what is happening in your life.

Elinor Hodges was ever so nasty about it. She said she thought it was disgusting the way people in television kept getting married and divorced all the time. She said she thought they were immoral and that marriage should be for ever.

It made me really upset, Elinor Hodges saying my mum was immoral. Sarah told me not to take any notice of her. She said, "Her mum and dad are religious nuts."

It is true that Elinor's parents are rather peculiar. They won't ever let her act in school plays and she always has to wear a scarf over her head, even though she is not a Muslim, but I think I sort of agree with her, just a little bit, about marriage being for ever.

I know people can't help falling out of love, any more than they can help falling in love. At least, I suppose they can't. It is difficult to be certain when I have never actually been in love myself, though I cannot imagine Darcey, for instance, ever not being my favourite dancer or Sarah not being my best friend.

But just because love cannot last for ever, I don't see that is any reason why people shouldn't go on living together. Lots of people live together that aren't in love. And then there wouldn't be all this horribleness that happens, with stories in the newspapers and people like Elinor Hodges telling you your mum is immoral.

I don't think Mum is immoral. I think that is a horrid thing to say. I think it is just that she is not very good at being married.

Elinor Hodges says lots of things are immoral. Music. Videos. Dancing. Kissing your boyfriend (if you have one). Sarah is right and I shouldn't take any notice of her.

I am not going to think about people like Elinor Hodges. I am trying to remember about the past.

And, of course, plan for the future!

9. My Cat Kitty

When your mum got married again, you left Bethnal Green and moved to a different part of London.

When Mum got married to Alan, we came to live in Kensington. "Out West," Uncle Eddy calls it.

It is nice out West and Alan was a nice dad (just for a short time). The house that we live in is a nice house. The garden is a nice garden. Everything is nice.

The house is very tall and thin, with attics that are real rooms that you can sleep in and a basement where there is a kitchen.

It has a garden with a wall round it, with spoke things stuck in the top so that the cats can't get out into the road and be run over.

There isn't any grass because it is not that sort of garden. Instead there are paving stones and lots of little trees, and plants growing in tubs.

I asked Mum if we could have Gran's toadstools when Gran died but Mum said there wasn't room for them. What she really meant was that she didn't like them. She never liked Gran's toadstools. She said they were as bad as garden gnomes.

I don't know what the matter is with garden gnomes! I think they are fun. I would like to have a pond with fish in it and gnomes sitting all around, smoking their little pipes and sitting in garden chairs underneath the toadstools. When I suggested this to Mum, she shuddered. She said, "Darling, don't be so vulgar!"

What is vulgar about it, I would like to know?

Mum says that Uncle Eddy is vulgar when he talks about needing a gypsy's or going to the bog. But Uncle Eddy just grins and makes a gesture with two of his fingers which is *really* vulgar. I know this for a fact because Sarah once did it to Elinor Hodges and Mrs Rowe saw her and nearly had a fit. I don't think Sarah realised that it is as terribly rude as it is.

It is funny how many things are rude that you don't know are rude until someone tells you off about them. Like once when I was little I saw this word written on a wall and I said it to Mum and she flew into the most furious rage and said that if ever she heard me say it again she would box my ears. She said that that was what came of having to live in Bethnal Green and let me mix with people like Stacey Kitchin.

That was ever so unfair. It wasn't Stacey's fault. She couldn't have said the word because she didn't even know how to read properly. She was still on her first reader when I was into real books. I wonder what has happened to Stacey?

She could be one of my guests!

I think nowadays that we have quite a lot of money. Mum has been in *Ask Auntie* for six years!!! It is shown in loads of other countries, including America, and when it is shown in other countries Mum gets a cheque. A *big* cheque if it's for America. When she gets a big cheque we go out and celebrate.

Last time she had one she took us to tea in a specially posh hotel in Piccadilly and I ate squishy cakes and buns with pink icing. Danny made a mess of everything as usual, dropping crumbs all over the floor. He is really too young to go to posh hotels. He doesn't know how to behave.

Mum said if he didn't learn better manners he wouldn't be able to come again.

It is nice having lots of money as it means we can buy clothes and go on holidays, which we never could before. It also means that I can have my own bedroom and can go to ballet classes with Miss Runcie. I adore Miss Runcie! When I am famous and on *This is Your*

Life I will tell everyone that it is because of her.

And also of course because of Violet.

We are very lucky to have so much money as it is much better than worrying all the time how the bills are to be paid. It is terrible, I think, to see people begging in the street because they have nowhere to live, especially if there is a child or a dog with them. I get upset when there is a child or a dog, thinking of them being cold and hungry. So I am very grateful that Mum is a success and I can go to Oakfield and learn ballet with Miss Runcie. I am definitely not complaining, but I still can't help remembering how it was when we lived with Gran.

I wish that Gran was here! I wish I could see her again, just once. I would far rather have Gran than new clothes and holidays. If I had a choice, that is. I would have my gran every time!

And Kitty.

I would have Kitty, as well. Bella and Bimbo are beautiful, but they are too superior to be cuddled. And they are Mum's cats. Kitty was mine. Well, she was Gran's really, but Gran always said she loved me best. I wanted to take her with us when we moved but Mum said it wouldn't be fair. She said that Kitty had lived with Gran all her life and she was too old to start again somewhere else.

She said, "She's seventeen, darling. It's a great age for a cat. She wouldn't be happy, in a new place."

I thought Mum was just making excuses. I thought she didn't want her because she had lost all her teeth and because she dribbled and sometimes bits of her fur came out. But Mum was right. When Gran died, Kitty missed her terribly. She came to live with us and she slept on my bed, but she pined. She wanted so much to be with Gran!

I hope Gran is right and that when you die you meet all the people who have gone before you. I would like to think of Kitty being with Gran again.

I cried oceans when Kitty died. Even more than when Gran did. I think it was because with Gran I knew that she wanted to go and be with Granddad, and so I knew that she was happy. But with Kitty, I couldn't be sure. Do animals meet up with their people or is it just for human beings? Heaven, I mean. If it's just for human beings, then where do the animals go?

I kept thinking of poor Kitty all on her own, without either me or Gran. I kept thinking how lost and lonely she would be, and I couldn't sleep for crying.

Mum got really worried. She said, "I knew we should have left her at the vet's instead of bringing her back home."

It was me that begged for Kitty to be brought home. I wanted her still to be with us. So Uncle Eddy came round and he took up one of the paving stones in the back garden and dug a hole and we made a proper little grave for her. Mum wrapped her in her favourite pink blanket and I kissed her goodbye and Uncle Eddy wrote "Kitty, a much loved cat. Aged 18 years 7 months" on the paving stone and painted some pawprints.

And then I cried and cried and couldn't stop, and that was when Mum went out and bought Bella and Bimbo, in the hope that they would comfort me.

I suppose they did, in a way. Kittens are very amusing and delightful, so that you cannot ignore them. Bimbo used to climb up the curtains, and Bella

ate Mum's house plants. It was really funny! You would pass her on the stairs carrying bits of plant in her mouth.

One year she climbed into the Christmas tree and tried to sit at the top of it as if she was a Christmas cat.

Mum was cross, because she fell off and ruined all the decorations. She said, "That cat! I'll have its guts for garters!"

But she didn't mean it. Mum loves her cats. I love them. too, but I still think about Kitty.

10. New School!

After you left Bethnal Green, you started at a new school.

It felt quite peculiar when I first went to Oakfield. Where I went in Bethnal Green, with Stacey Kitchin, there were boys. At Oakfield there are only girls. Mum said she thought this was a good thing. She said, "Boys would only distract you."

Uncle Eddy winks and says, "What she means is, boys distracted *her*!"

Mum had heaps of boyfriends when she was young. She was always having battles with Gran because Gran thought some of her boyfriends were unsuitable and because Mum used to defy her by staying out later than she should have done.

I wonder if I will ever have a boyfriend? Uncle Eddy says, "You bet you will! Dozens of 'em!" But sometimes I am not sure.

Sarah has one. Sort of. He is a friend of her brother Barney. He is fourteen and very handsome, or so Sarah says. I have never seen him. She has only met him twice, once at her brother's party and once when she went to their school's sports day with her mum. But at least it is a start.

I have never even met a boy. Not properly. Sarah says if I didn't spend so much time at ballet classes I could get out and about and do other things and that way, perhaps, I would extend my social life, but all I want is to become a dancer!

It is quite posh at Oakfield Manor. Lots of the people there have parents who are seriously rich. Mum and Uncle Eddy sometimes have arguments about it. Uncle Eddy says Mum is a class traitor and should be ashamed of herself. For sending me to a posh school, he means. He says it sort of jokingly, but at the same time I think he is a little bit serious.

Mum always retorts that she doesn't want a daughter of hers going to a dump like she had to go to, and then Uncle Eddy says that she hasn't done so badly for someone who went to a dump, and Mum says, "No, but I've had to fight every inch of the way. I want to give my kids all the advantages that I never had." She says that if Uncle Eddy had kids, he would feel the same.

I don't know whether he would. He is very fierce about that sort of thing. Politics, and that.

On the other hand, when he came to see me and Zoë one time, and afterwards I was telling him about Zoë's mum being really poor and how it didn't seem fair that some people had simply loads of money while others had none, he told me not to worry myself too much about it because it was "just the way of the world".

I said that I didn't worry all the time, only just now and again when I was with someone like Zoë and it made me think about things, and he said, "Don't think too much. Just concentrate on being happy." I said, "But *you* think." And then I asked him whether he really believed that it was wrong for me to go to Oakfield and be privileged, which is what he once told Mum that I was, and he looked sort of... stricken. I think that's the word. And he put both his arms round me and hugged me really hard and said, "Little Becky, you grab all the privileges you can."

So maybe it's all right. Even if it isn't, there is nothing I can do about it. You have to go to the schools that you are told to go to. And I would hate to leave Oakfield now!

This is partly because I am used to it and partly because of Sarah. We have been best friends almost since that first moment in the playground when she called me Becky Bananas. That is a long time! Other people quarrel and stop being friends, but Sarah and I don't like quarrelling. Sarah's mum and dad do it all night long, from the minute her dad gets in to the minute they fall asleep. Sometimes they do it right round till morning. Sarah has heard them. She finds it quite upsetting and that is why she never does it herself. She just laughs if people try to quarrel with her.

I don't quarrel, because of not having any bottle. If I'd got bottle I'd have said something to Elinor Hodges for calling my mum immoral. That is a hateful thing to say about someone's mum. I bet Sarah would have said something. She wouldn't have quarrelled, but she would have said something. I wish that I had!

I like going to Oakfield. I even like wearing the uniform, which some people think is naff.

It is bright red, and I think that is far more interesting than brown or navy, which is what most schools have. I like the little waistcoats, as well; I think they are cute. I even like the Latin motto on our blazer pockets.

It means, through hard work to the stars. The stars are what I am aiming for! But it is true that you have to work hard to reach them.

Doing ballet is *very* hard work. I can't wait to get back to it! Every day that I'm not taking class is a day lost from my life. Miss Runcie says, "Don't worry, you're still young and flexible. You'll catch up." But soon I will be twelve, and twelve is not young! Not for ballet.

I can't afford to waste any more time. I must go back to class *immediately*.

It is no use thinking about ballet just at the moment. I am thinking about Oakfield now. I am thinking about what a good school it is and how lucky I am to go there. That is what I am thinking about.

We do lots of interesting things at Oakfield. School plays, for instance. And carol concerts, where we raise money for charity. We all get to vote which charity we're going to do it for. Sometimes it's children, sometimes it's animals, sometimes it's for people that are starving. There was a picture in the school magazine last Christmas of Elinor Hodges presenting the cheque. She only got chosen because she had less order marks than anyone else. In fact she didn't have any at all, which is because she never does anything wrong. Sarah says it's sickening, but I suppose she can't help it. It's just the way she is.

Sarah gets order marks for being cheeky and answering back. (A bit like Mum!) I get order marks for being what Sarah calls "daffy". By this she means that I sometimes daydream instead of paying attention so that when I am asked questions I haven't any idea what the teacher has been asking me, and as a result I give these really silly dumb replies. And then I get given order marks!

What I daydream about, mostly, is being on stage with Darcey. She might be dancing Princess Aurora, for example, and I will be dancing the Lilac Fairy.

Or she will be Swanhilda and I will be one of her Friends.

Or maybe we will be in *Sylphides* together.

Those are the sort of things I dream about.

Per ardua ad astra! Nothing that is worth getting is got easily. That is what Uncle Eddy says.

11. I Meet a Famous Author (and Write a Book)

Something quite exciting happened to you at Oakfield.
Yes! We had a Book Week and I met this
famous author.

Last year, it was. We had this Book Week. A person came from a publisher's to tell us all about how books were made and an author came to tell us how she writes her stories, and at the end of the week we all dressed up as Characters from Literature and did a quiz. I got two prizes! One was for dressing up as Pocahontas (I would really like to have dressed up as Posy, from *Ballet Shoes*, but I didn't think anyone would recognise me) and the other was for coming second in the quiz. I was given two book tokens and I spent them on a book about Darcey!!!

When I got the prize for being Pocahontas I

heard Greta Lundquist whisper to Susie Smith, "You know why they gave it to *her*?" and I saw Susie nod. They weren't being nasty, or anything. I mean, they didn't know that I could hear. But I wondered if that was what everyone else was thinking and if I really had only been given the prize because of people feeling sorry for me.

I don't want people to feel sorry for me! It is horrid when you think that they are looking at you and thinking things.

I would like to ask Sarah if she thinks things, but I am too much of a coward. Zoë is the only person I can talk to about it. She is the only one who understands. And Zoë agrees with me. *We do not want people to feel sorry for us.*

Except ourselves, because sometimes you can't help it, though I try hard not to. I think that self-pity is a negative emotion. It doesn't lead to anything positive but just to tears, which makes you feel worse.

The author who came to our Book Week was a lady called Jane Rue. There are some of her books in the library but I had never read any before she came. Then we did one in class and it was quite funny so that I was looking forward to the visit, though some people groaned and said that it would be a dead bore.

Susie said, "An *author*. Yuck!" and screwed up her nose.

Someone else said, "I'd rather do maths!" Other people got fussed in case she wanted us to write things, but Mrs Rowe said all she was going to do was talk to us and tell us about her books, and then we would be expected to ask questions. So Elinor Hodges immediately went away and prepared a huge long list that would have taken about ten days if she'd asked all of them.

Before Jane Rue came, we speculated what she would look like. Sarah said she would be old, because authors were always old. Andrea Francis thought she would be rich and arrive in a Rolls-Royce. I didn't know what to expect, never having seen an author before, but I thought she would probably be very smart with high heels and a handbag and maybe wearing a fur coat, though hopefully not a real one.

I was so amazed when she came walking into the hall behind Mrs Rowe and Mrs Rowe introduced her! I couldn't believe that she was an author! She just looked completely ordinary, like a person that you might meet anywhere. She was older than Mum but not old, like Gran was old. She didn't have grey hair. And she wasn't dressed in the least bit smartly, just in jeans and a sweater, without a fur of any kind. She didn't have a handbag, either – or high heels! All she had was a huge big shoulder bag containing lots of books.

She dumped all the books on a table, and out of the corner of my eye I could see Susie pulling faces. Susie doesn't go for books. She reckons they're dinosaur material. But I quite like reading, and so I was interested. Had this author really written so many?

She had! She had written *dozens*. I couldn't imagine where she would get all her ideas from, but she said that that was what she was going to tell us.

She said that she started writing when she was little because she was very shy and couldn't make any friends. So that was why she started writing. She made up her own friends and put them into books.

She said that the very first book she ever had published was a book about a girl who becomes a dancer. That made me sit up! She said that she always desperately wanted to be a dancer herself but that her mum and dad couldn't afford for her to have lessons and so she became very unhappy and frustrated. So then one day when she was about fifteen she thought she would write a book about a girl who wanted to learn ballet, and so she wrote this book called

Castanets & Ballet Shoes, in which the girl becomes hugely successful, and guess what? She ends up dancing Odette!

I was *really* interested in that. Everyone turned round to look at me and I could feel myself growing bright scarlet. Mrs Rowe said, "We have our own little ballerina here," which truly embarrassed me. I could have fallen through the floor! Fancy calling me a ballerina! When I'm not yet even a member of the corps de ballet! But people that aren't dancers don't understand.

The more this author talked to us, the more I realised that she wasn't as ordinary as she looked. She was a very amusing and witty person. She told us, for example, how she and her husband had all these animals that they had rescued. Pigs and goats and chickens. And two Shetland ponies and some sheep. Not to mention fifteen cats and six dogs!!!

She showed us pictures of the cats and dogs and told us how they spoke, using different voices. Susie, thinking she was being very clever, put up her hand and said, "Excuse me, but animals can't talk," and the author said, "Excuse me, but mine can!"

She told us how, if you listened very carefully and took the trouble to get to know them and to really

understand them, then
you would hear them
talking. It is true! Bella
and Bimbo talk all the
time. They are very
superior and have upper-
class voices like the
Queen.

I don't think Kitty would have had an upper-class
voice. I think she would speak what Mum calls
"common". But I still love her best!

Another thing the author told us was that all the
dogs slept in the bedroom with her and her husband,
and that four of them actually slept in the bed so that
they had to have this really huge great bed taking up
most of the room. I could hardly believe what I was
hearing. Four dogs sleeping in bed with you!

We were all giggling like crazy because some of the
stuff this author was telling us was really funny, like
about this one dog, Benny, that is a deaf dog and looks
like a walking hearth rug and sleeps in the middle of
the bed with his head on the pillow. She said he has
this habit of suddenly standing up underneath the
duvet so that all the cold air comes billowing in. And
then he starts shaking his head so that his ears go flap

flap flap and the cold air whirls all about. And then when he has done that he starts turning in circles and trampling up and down as he makes a nest for himself. And the duvet goes in circles with him so that in the end he is all wrapped up in it like a big walnut whip and she and her husband are left without any.

Everyone laughed at this except for Elinor Hodges. Even Susie laughed. You could tell that Elinor was being all disapproving and thinking that it was not hygienic to let dogs sleep in the bed and that dogs should be kept outside in kennels. Which is what I personally do not agree with, and neither would the author have done because she was a real animal person.

She told us that some people thought she was mad, but that she didn't care. She said, "Some of you probably think I'm mad," and she looked at Susie as she said it. And Susie turned pink and couldn't think what to say, which is the first time I have ever known her to be at a loss for words!

At the end we were told we could ask questions, so Elinor Hodges at once stood up with her great long list and started asking these really dreary, boring sort of questions such as "How long does it take you to write a book?" and "Do you have a word processor?"

The author said she didn't use a word processor, she always wrote her first draft by hand and then typed it out on an ordinary typewriter. She said, "I'm afraid I'm a bit of a technological dinosaur."

Susie turned round at this and made an "I-told-you-so" face at me and Sarah. But then the next minute she was waving her hand in the air to ask a question and the question was, "How much do you earn?"

Mrs Rowe was absolutely furious! She told Susie off for being impertinent and vulgar, though the author didn't seem to mind. She explained to us that she didn't earn a fortune and that hardly any authors did. She said, "You don't write books for the money, you write them because you feel you have to," and Susie raised her eyebrows right up into her hair as if the author was a bit simple, or something. Susie is really into making money. She understands all about stocks and shares and compound interest, which to me is just boring.

When I got home I told Mum all about the visit and about the author having all these animals and four dogs sleeping in the bed, and Mum said that she was obviously mad.

I told Mum that lots of people thought she was mad but that the author didn't care, and I said that I personally thought it would be lovely to have four dogs sleeping in bed with you. You could cuddle them and never get cold, and if you woke up and felt a bit lonely or frightened there would always be someone to lick you or snuggle up to.

Mum cried, "Oh, darling!" and held out her arms. She said that if I ever woke up and felt lonely I could go into her room and sleep in bed with her. She said, "You can snuggle up to me any time you like. You know that."

I do know it, but it seems childish at my age to sleep with your mum.

After the author had been to visit us I wrote to her telling her how totally brilliant her talk had been and how interested I was in her having wanted to be a dancer because I hoped to be a dancer myself one day. She wrote this long letter back, which I still have. I will never get rid of it! It is a precious object. Right at the end she wished me luck and said that she would watch out for my name on the posters.

So that is two famous people who are going to watch out for me! Jane Rue and Darcey.

When I am on *This is Your Life* I very much hope

that Ms Rue will be a guest because then I can tell her how her visit inspired me.

One of the other things she said in her letter was that I used words very well and that maybe one day I would write a story myself. "A ballet story, perhaps." She said, "It was a great comfort to me when I wrote *Castanets & Ballet Shoes*. It didn't stop me yearning to be a dancer, but it took away some of my frustration." She said that writing is a very good way of exploring your emotions and can be a great solace.

I thought about what she said and last term I wrote this book about a girl called Bryony who wants to be a dancer only she gets ill with AML and has to go into hospital and have drugs and everyone thinks she is going to die, but she doesn't. Instead she goes into remission and starts at the Royal Ballet School when she is twelve years old and when she is seventeen she is taken into the Company and dances in *Swan Lake*. She dances Odette and everyone applauds and she is given a big bouquet of flowers and that is how it ends.

The book is thirty-five pages long. I typed it out on the word processor with wide margins and double-spacing, like Jane Rue said you had to. She said that publishers cannot read handwriting, they can only read typing. I don't know why this is. Perhaps their eyesight is poor because of all the books they have to look at.

I had to use the word processor when Mum was out as the book is *A Secret*! There is only one person I have shown it to, and that is Uncle Eddy. He thinks it is good enough to be published, maybe, but I am not sure about this. For one thing I don't think the spelling is quite right, though Uncle Eddy says that doesn't matter. He says the publishers would see to it. He says the only thing that I would have to do is to explain about AML, as not everyone will know what it is.

I would have to explain that it is *acute myeloid leukaemia* and that acute means it is not something that goes on for years and years just the same but is something that happens quite quickly, like for instance a pimple that comes to a head and bursts, and that myeloid is to do with bone marrow, and that leukaemia is a sort of cancer that attacks the blood.

When you go into remission it means that the drugs have worked and you don't have it any more, but sometimes the remission doesn't last and then you have to go and have more drugs.

People that know about it, like doctors, or people that have got it, quite often just call it AML. There are lots of other sorts, but AML is what Bryony has got. It is not as common as the other sorts except in older people, so that Bryony is a bit unusual. Most children that have leukaemia have the other sorts.

I called my heroine Bryony because I think it is a nice-sounding name and good for a ballet dancer. It is a kind of flower, as a matter of fact, which grows in hedges.

Mum showed it to me once when we were out for a walk and I thought that it was pretty. I didn't know then that I would be writing a book about it!

Born to Dance by Becky Banaras

Born to Dance

This is the story of Bryony in the book that I wrote.

One day when Bryony wakes up she has a pain in her leg. She tells her mum and her mum says she has probably strained it. "Doing all those ballet exercises." Bryony thinks that maybe it was when she was doing *grands battements*.

But she thinks she will be able to work her way through it, because quite often that is what dancers do when they have aches and pains. So that afternoon when she goes to class she tries to pretend that everything is the same as usual and to forget about her leg and how it is hurting.

But next day it is worse and when she goes for class her teacher notices and says to her that she must rest for a while and not come to class until it is better. She says that she has probably pulled a muscle and it is best to rest it.

Bryony really hates to miss class but her leg is so bad she can hardly bear to walk on it. Also she is feeling quite tired and people start to say how pale she is.

At first her mum doesn't worry because she has always been pale. Once at school some unkind girls made a nickname for her and the nickname was "Pasty". But then one morning Bryony wakes up and she has a pain in her other leg as well, and now her mum starts to get a bit anxious and tells the au pair to take her to the doctor. Bryony's mum cannot go to the doctor with her as she has to be at work. She is a big television star and they are doing some important filming, but the au pair, who is called Rosa-Maria, is quite nice. Bryony doesn't mind going to the doctor with her.

The doctor is also quite nice. He has been to see Bryony before, when she has had mumps and chickenpox. He says to

Rosa-Maria that she must take Bryony immediately to the hospital to have a blood test so that they can find out what is wrong.

The blood test means having a needle stuck in her arm and a tube of blood sucked out, which is not very pleasant, but Bryony is eleven and so she is brave about it.

When her mum comes home that day she cannot understand why Bryony has had to go to the hospital to have the blood sucked out. She says, "Why does she need to have blood sucked out for a pulled muscle?" Rosa-Maria says that the doctor thinks maybe Bryony might be anaemic. (Which is something else Uncle Eddy said I would have to explain.)

Anaemic means not having enough red blood cells which carry the oxygen round your body and give you energy. If people don't have enough red cells, then they get tired.

At six o'clock that night the doctor rings up and speaks to Bryony's mum. He says he has had the result of the blood test and would like to come round to discuss it.

Bryony's mum turns pale. She says, "I hope it isn't anything serious?" But the doctor won't tell her until he comes.

When the doctor arrives, Bryony is told to go and watch television with Rosa-Maria and her little brother Joseph. She doesn't hear what the doctor says, but afterwards, when he has gone, she sees that her mum has been crying. Her mum tells her that she is anaemic and that is why she has felt tired. She says that she has to go back to the hospital so that the doctors can find out what is causing it.

When they go to the hospital a second time it is a different hospital, it is a hospital that deals only with children, and Bryony's mum goes with her. Bryony is glad that it is her mum and not Rosa-Maria. She likes Rosa-Maria but it is not the same as being with her mum.

At the hospital they are taken to a room with four beds in it. Two of the beds are empty but in one bed there is a girl of about Bryony's age. She is sitting up against the pillows and listening to music through headphones. She is very pretty with blonde hair and a red nightdress with white dots. She smiles at Bryony but Bryony is too frightened to smile back. What has frightened her is that this girl has plastic tubes coming out of her nightdress. The tubes are stuck to the side of the bed and are attached to plastic bags that hang off a metal stand.

You can see inside the plastic bags. One of them has something that looks like blood in it. Bryony feels sick and scared. Is this what is going to happen to her?

The girl takes off her headphones and says, "Hi! I'm Chloë. Are you a new patient?"

Bryony is too scared to say anything at all so her mum has to say it for her. Bryony is a bit of a coward. She hasn't any bottle. She is even scared of being X-rayed! This is silly, because X-rays don't hurt. But then she has to have an injection so that the doctor can take a sample of her bone marrow. He has to punch a needle into her hip, and that is nasty. That is *really* nasty. Her mum tells her to be brave and Bryony tries hard but she is scared and trembling all the time even though her mum is with her.

After that she is taken back to the room with the four beds and she has to get into one of the beds and have blood dripped into her from a plastic bag hanging from a metal stand, just like the girl called Chloë, except that Bryony only has one plastic bag. While Bryony's mum is outside talking to the doctor, Chloë tells Bryony that she'll probably have lots once they start treatment.

Bryony is horrified to discover that she is going to have to stay in the hospital. She had thought she was going home! She says to her mum, "But what about my dancing classes?" and her mum has to explain to her that she can't have dancing classes for the moment. She says, "You have to wait until you're better."

Bryony asks how long that will be and her mum looks grave and says, "It could be a month or two."

That is the *worst* news.

It is only later that her mum tells her what is wrong with her. She tells her that she has AML and that the doctors are going to give her drugs that will cure it.

After Bryony's mum has gone and Bryony and Chloë are alone, Chloë tells Bryony that she has leukaemia as well, only hers is a different sort. Hers is called ALL. ALL stands for *acute lymphoblastic leukaemia*. She says that to begin with she couldn't ever remember the word *lymphoblastic* but that now she can. But she doesn't know what it means! Not properly. The doctor has told her, but she can't make sense of it. It is too complicated.

Chloë says that ALL is what most children have. Not so many have what Bryony has got. Bryony doesn't know whether this is a good thing or a bad thing, but Chloë tells her not to worry. She says, "They can almost always cure it nowadays. They just give you chemo and then you go into remission."

Bryony is so ignorant she doesn't know what chemo is or what remission means! Chloë tells her that chemo is chemotherapy and means drugs. She says, "They make you feel sick but it's worth it if it puts you into remission." She says that remission is when the leukaemia goes away and you don't feel tired any more or get bruises.

Bryony says that she never got bruises, she just got pains in her legs. Chloë says that what she got was headaches and a high temperature. But she says that it's different for everyone. Chloë has been in the hospital for a few days and already seems to know everything.

It helps Bryony, having Chloë there to talk to. They become best friends. Best *hospital* friends. When one of them is sad the other cheers her up, or if one of them is frightened the other makes her brave. Chloë has lots more bottle than Bryony but even Chloë gets frightened sometimes.

After a few weeks Bryony is allowed to go home because she is in remission, which means there are no more cancer cells in her blood. Everyone is happy and Bryony's mum takes her to have a special tea at a smart hotel to celebrate. The hotel is in the West End. It is full of palm trees and beautiful blue carpet and Bryony eats cream cakes, as many as she likes.

She is not worried about being too fat for ballet because she has lost lots of weight and the doctor says she must try to put it on again.

She is told that she can go back to her ballet classes but not as many as before.

Only one a week to begin with. But one a week is not enough! Her mum says, "Give it a while and we'll see."

She still has to have chemo and all her hair is falling out. This is because of the drugs. Chloë's hair has fallen out, too. It happens to most people, but Bryony knows that it will grow again. The doctor has told her so.

One day when Bryony goes to the hospital for her blood test they tell her that she is no longer in remission. The leukaemia has come back and she must go into hospital again. She is very ill and her mum cries and so does Rosa-Maria because they think she is going to die. Everyone thinks she is going to die. Even the doctors and nurses. They think they are hiding it from her but she knows what they are thinking. When her Uncle Ted comes to visit her, she tells him that this is what they think and he says to her, "What do you think?"

Bryony says, "I'm not going to die! I'm going to get better and become a famous dancer!"

And Uncle Ted says, "If that's what you believe, then that's what will happen."

And it does, and everyone is amazed because they didn't think it was possible.

She dances Odette and is famous and that is the end.

THE END
A book by Rebecca Banaras

Uncle Eddy says the best bit is where Bryony says she's not going to die and she doesn't. He says that most of the book is sad and makes you weep, but that the ending is "brave and beautiful". He says that

it ought to be published because it would give hope to
other children that have got leukaemia.

He means children like me.

13. The Bad Times

When you were ten years old, something happened
and you had to go into hospital.

The same as Bryony. I have got what Bryony's got. I suppose, really, that's what made me write the book.

Uncle Eddy is the only person who has read it. I can't show it to Mum because she would start crying. Mum cries very easily. And Sarah wouldn't like it because she doesn't like anything to do with illness. She likes to pretend it isn't happening.

I can't even show it to Zoë. Zoë is the same as Chloë in my book. Chloë is her.

Zoë was the one who told me right at the beginning that you have to stay in remission for five years before you are properly cured. If you come out of remission before that time, then you probably won't ever be cured.

The sooner you come out of remission, the worse the prognosis is. That is what Zoë told me.

Prognosis is just a word which means outlook. Like, the outlook is good. Or the outlook is bleak.

If you come out of remission in the first year, then the outlook is very bleak.

That is what Zoë told me. Right at the beginning, when I didn't even know what chemo was.

I don't know how she found out about all these things. Asked the doctors, I expect. Zoë always wants to find out about everything. She's ever so much braver than me.

She'll come on my programme for sure!

Zoë is like a lion! The only thing that really upsets her is not seeing her dad.

The first time Uncle Eddy came to visit me, Zoë went and buried herself under the bedclothes and wouldn't come out. When he'd gone I heard her crying. I'd never heard her cry before. Not even when they stuck a tube in her chest so that the drugs could be dripped straight in without having to be injected. She really didn't want them to do that but she still didn't cry. But she cried that day when Uncle Eddy came.

When I asked her what the matter was she said, "It's all right for you, you've got a dad!" She thought Uncle Eddy was my dad! I didn't know then that Zoë's dad never came to see her. Her mum came as often as she could but even her mum couldn't come every day because she lives out in Essex and she couldn't always afford it. So that was when I decided to share Uncle Eddy with her. I think it cheered her up a bit to know that I hadn't got a dad, either.

We were in hospital for ages together, me and Zoë. They couldn't get us into remission. With some people it happens almost at once, but with me and Zoë it took weeks. And then Zoë went and got sick with this infection, which was the only time her dad ever came to visit her.

It was horrid when she had the infection because they separated us and I wasn't allowed to see her in case I caught whatever it was. I missed her so much! We always told each other everything, Zoë and me. We used to compare notes about what the doctor had said and what the results of our blood tests were and how we were both doing. And now I was on my own!

They put another girl in Zoë's bed. She was only little, only about seven years old; she didn't know what was happening. She kept screaming whenever the nurses came to take blood samples.

I felt sorry for her, but she was too young to talk to the way I could talk to Zoë. I was terrified in case Zoë didn't come back. Or in case she died and they didn't tell me.

I knew that people died. There was this little boy called Kris that was only a baby. He was only about Danny's age. He died. A girl that was there, a big girl called Amanda, she tried to tell us that he had gone home. I believed her. It was Zoë found out what had really happened. She found out that he had died. Zoë always finds things out. She's like a magpie. Inquisitive. But she says it's better to know than not.

I suppose she is right.

My favourite nurse is Carol. I'd want her to be on the programme!

149

She used to be on nights, but now she's on days so I see more of her.

When Zoë had her infection, Carol knew that I was frightened. She told me not to worry, that Zoë was going to be all right. And she promised to make sure she was put back in the same bed.

I wanted to believe her! But Zoë had already warned me about them not always telling the truth. She said that when she first came, there had been someone else in my bed. There had been a girl called Trudi. One day she had disappeared and not come back and Ellen, who is another nurse, told Zoë that she had gone into remission. It was only later Zoë discovered she had died. So I still went on worrying, until one afternoon I woke up and there was Zoë, grinning at me from the next bed. She said, "I'm back!" and Carol said, "I told you so," and I felt mean for not trusting her.

Zoë said, "Why feel mean?" She said, "They lie all the time. I can't stand being lied to!"

I don't think they lie, exactly. I think they just want to protect us. They don't want to tell us bad things unless they absolutely have to. They think we will find it upsetting, knowing that people the same age as us are dying. But as Zoë says, we're not babies. When you're eleven, you know what's going on.

I think personally it would be a comfort if you knew you could always rely on them, the doctors and the nurses. And parents, as well. If you knew that they would tell you the truth. That way it would mean you wouldn't get to worry quite so much.

This is why Zoë and me made a pact that we would always tell each other what was happening and not smile brightly and say everything was all right if it wasn't. Like if we'd just had a bad result from a blood test, we would tell each other. Which we always did.

When we had been having chemo for a few weeks, our hair started falling out. Zoë's started first, because she'd been having chemo longer than me. She said, "It doesn't happen to everybody. Maybe you'll be lucky." But then I woke up one morning and found bits of hair all scattered about the pillow and I knew that it was happening.

I kept trying to pretend to myself that it wasn't but every time I brushed my hair the brush would be all full of it, and I kept looking at Zoë and seeing these bald patches and I just couldn't bear it, the thought that I was going to end up looking like that.

Zoë did her best to make me brave. She said things like, "It's only temporary," and "It's only hair," and "What does it matter so long as we're going to get better?" She said that lots of children with leukaemia get completely cured. "But they have to lose their hair first."

I wailed, "But I grew mine long, specially! Specially for ballet! It took me ages!"

Zoë said, "It'll all come back again. Mine did."

At first I didn't realise what she was saying, but then I said, "What do you mean, yours did?" And then she told me, she'd had chemo before. She'd had it when she was seven years old. She said, "I've been in remission all this time. Almost five years! If you're in remission for five years, they reckon you're cured."

Another few months, and Zoë would have been cured. But she said she wasn't worried. She said, "The longer you stay in remission, the better your chances are." She said if she'd only been in remission for a month or so, then she would know that she was probably going to die. But as it was, she was going to go back into remission and this time she was going to stay in remission and when she grew up she was going to be a nurse and come and look after other children that had leukaemia.

"Because then I'll be able to tell them that I've been through it."

We talked a lot about what we are going to do when

we're grown up. Zoë said that when I was a famous dancer I would have to come and visit her in her hospital ward and talk to all the children with leukaemia and tell them that I'd been through it, as well. I promised that I would. We agreed that it would be nice if some well-known person that had had leukaemia and their hair had fallen out would come back and talk to us. It would cheer you up.

There must be *some* well-known people that have had it.

Mum told me that there is a famous singer called something I can't remember, something Spanish, and that he has had it, but it is not the same because he had it when he was grown up, not when he was a child. And I don't know whether his hair fell out or not. Maybe it doesn't if you are grown up. Or maybe it had fallen out anyway, like Mr Tucker's at school, simply because he is old. It wouldn't be so bad if you were old. It is horrid when you are still young.

It's not only hair falling out, it's other things, too. Like your mouth getting sore and your gums bleeding so you can't clean your teeth properly. And people sticking needles into you all the time to take samples or give you drugs. Some of the drugs are foul, they make you feel really ill, and some of them make your skin burn. Zoë said she didn't have to have these ones when she was only seven but they were giving them to her now because of her having relapsed, which is what it is called when you come out of remission.

These are the ones that made me cry. I told Uncle Eddy I didn't want them any more and he held me and let me weep over him and said that I was his brave girl. But I'm not! I'm not in the least bit brave! I haven't any bottle at all. I hate it!

Even Zoë hated it when her skin got burnt. It's really painful. But Zoë never cries. She just gets cross and swears. I wish I was more like Zoë.

Something that happened to me and not to her was nosebleeds. I've had dozens of them. I've had so many I've sometimes thought they're never going to stop. Once I bled all over a picture of Darcey, in a book that Mum gave me for Christmas. That made me cry again, when that happened. It seemed so terrible, to nosebleed over Darcey. Zoë tried to rub her clean for me but there were still all these horrible browny smears.

When mum came to visit me she couldn't understand why I was so weepy, and when I showed her the picture she said, "Oh, darling! Don't worry about that. I'll buy you another copy." But I still felt awful. I hate my body doing all these horrible, disgusting things and me not having any control over it.

I've tried explaining this to Mum but all she says is, "That's the problem with being a dancer. You expect too much of yourself. You ask the impossible."

She says there are times when you can't expect to have control. She said, "Like, for instance, when I was pregnant with you... there you were, growing away inside me, and me getting fatter and fatter, and not a thing I could do about it except just wait for you to get big enough to come popping out."

That is true, but Mum *wanted* to have me. I didn't want to have AML. I didn't want to get sick and bald and bleed all over Darcey! Mum had a baby to look forward to, but what have I got?

Mum says that I've got the future. She says, "That's what you must hold on to. You're putting up with all this now, so that in the future you can be well and strong. Whenever you feel low, you just keep reminding yourself."

I do try, but sometimes it's not easy. Sometimes it seems as if I'm just saying it to myself and it doesn't really mean anything. Sometimes I think I'll never be well and strong.

It was better when Zoë was here. I felt braver when I had her to talk to.

Zoë got out of hospital before me. She went back into remission and they let her go home. She promised she'd come and visit me, and she did for a little while, because she still had to come back to the hospital once a week for tests, but then I went into remission as well and we didn't see each other very much after that. Only just now and again when we had an appointment on the same day, except once when Uncle Eddy had to drive down to Essex and he took me with him and left me at Zoë's and we spent the day together.

We went up to her bedroom and looked at ourselves in the mirror and giggled because Zoë said, "We're like a pair of boiled eggs!"

Usually I didn't look like an egg because I wore my wig that Mum bought for me. It's a special one made out of real hair the same colour as mine, so that nobody at school ever knew that really I was bald. But Zoë's mum couldn't afford a wig, so when I went to her place I didn't wear mine. I took it off and left it in the car so as not to upset her.

Lots of children, when their hair has fallen out, they wear scarves, but Zoë is too proud. She just went walking round bald and didn't care who saw her. "It's trendy," she said. "It's the new fashion." I think that is *really* brave.

I am too vain, I suppose.

14. Jokes!

At last, you went into remission.

We had celebrations when I came out of hospital. Uncle Eddy came and we all went for a meal, me and Mum and Uncle Eddy. We left Danny at home with Ana-Maria, who's our au pair, because he is too young. He is just a silly nuisance in a restaurant.

Mum bought pink champagne, and we all got to drink it. Even I was allowed a glass!

Mum and Uncle Eddy toasted to me. They clinked glasses and said, "To Becky!" Then Uncle Eddy winked and said, "Here's looking at you, kid!"

As a matter of fact, everyone in the restaurant was looking at Mum. They always do. She can't go anywhere without being looked at. But that evening she didn't mind. She was really happy! She hugged me and said, "Darling, I know the drugs are perfectly horrid, but you see, it has been worth it, hasn't it? Now you can concentrate on getting strong again!"

All I wanted to do was start back on my ballet

classes. Dr Stanhope, who is my doctor that looks after me at the hospital, said that I could do one class a week but that I was to stop if I got tired. Mum was scared it would be too much for me, but Dr Stanhope talked to me about it and I told him how I was going to be a dancer when I grew up and how important it was to me to have classes, and he spoke to Mum and then it was all right.

I really like Dr Stanhope! He is another person I will have on my programme.

He is a person who understands. He told Mum that if ballet meant so much to me, then I must be allowed to do it.

Uncle Eddy agreed with him. I heard him talking to Mum when they didn't know I was there. He said, "I know it's difficult for you, kid." He calls Mum kid just like he calls me, even though she's older than he is. He said, "I know the temptation to wrap her in cotton wool, but she's got to be allowed to live her life."

Uncle Eddy understands as well! I don't think Mum always does, or maybe it's just that she worries more. Every week when I had to come back to the hospital for tests she would ring up from the studios to check if everything was all right. She said she couldn't concentrate properly until she knew.

Ana-Maria used to bring me to the hospital. I would have rather it was Mum, but on the other hand at least Ana-Maria never got nervous, like Mum did when she came. When Mum came she gave me the jitters. I didn't have the jitters as a rule because I was used to it. Also, I knew everybody. People used to say hello to me. The nurses and the doctors and the men with the trolleys.

And sometimes Zoë would be here and then we would have fun, giggling together.

me + zoe

I always giggle with Zoë. When I am a dancer and she is a nurse and I go back to visit her to talk to her patients, we will probably still giggle. She is the sort of person you can't help giggling with.

I haven't got anyone to giggle with now. Now that I'm back in the hospital. I just lie here and think. What I think about mostly is dancing *Swan Lake*. I dance it in my head and imagine that I am on stage. So long as I can imagine that, I am all right.

It is just sometimes, when it stops being real and I know that I am only dreaming it, that I get frightened. Time is rushing past and I am missing all my classes. I should be having at least three a week! I haven't had any for at least two months. How am I going to be a dancer if I can't have classes? And my hair was growing back and now it's all starting to fall out again and I hate these horrible drugs that make me feel sick, I feel sick, sick, sick all of the time and my mouth hurts and I'm having nosebleeds again and sometimes I think that I am going to die.

Sometimes I think that I wouldn't mind dying if it meant no more of the horrible drugs.

But I am not going to! I am going to live to be a hundred!

I am going to be like Bryony and dance in *Swan Lake*. And then they will say *Leukaemia girl beats illness to become ballerina*. That is the sort of thing that they say. And there will be interviews on radio and television and in the magazines. People will come to the theatre, to my dressing room, to talk to me and write articles, like they do with Mum. But unlike Mum I will not be recognised all over the place in supermarkets or when I am walking down the street as not so many people recognise ballet dancers. Lots of girls at school didn't even recognise Darcey until I told them who she was!

That is incredible, not recognising Darcey. Everyone recognises television stars. That is because more people watch television than go to the ballet. But that is all right. I don't specially want to be recognised. I just want to dance!

I have got to get better *quickly* or it will be too late.

I am trying to think of some jokes.

What did one magnet say to the other magnet?

"I find you attractive."

Ha ha. That is not very funny.

Where did the Vikings drink?

At a Norse trough.

Neither is that. They are the sort of jokes you find in Christmas crackers.

I have just remembered one that someone told me yesterday.

This is the joke. There's this boy who's just started at a new school. The teacher asks him if he can read and write. He says, "I can write, but I can't read." So the teacher says, "All right. Here's a piece of paper. Show me how you write your name." So the boy writes something on the paper and the teacher picks it up and looks at it and it is just scribble. "What's this?" she says. And the boy says, "How should I know? I told you, I can't read."

Ho ho! That is a really stupid one.

I'm not very good with jokes as I can never remember the end of them. Well, hardly ever. I only remembered this one because it's so stupid. Zoë used to tell me lots, only hers were really funny.

I wish she was here now and then I could ask her to tell them to me again. This time I might be able to remember the endings and then I could tell them to someone else.

There is a girl in the bed opposite who would probably like to hear some jokes. This is the first time she has been in hospital and she keeps crying for her mum. Her auntie is with her but her mum is in hospital as well. I think that is so sad. I would like to be able to cheer her up.

Maybe when Uncle Eddy comes I will ask him to go over and tell her some jokes. He is good at making people laugh. But I don't know when he is going to be able to come. He is in Africa.

He sent me a card with lions on it.

On the back he wrote, "Here's looking at you, kid!" He is always saying that, I don't know why. But I like it when he says it.

I hope he comes back soon! I want him to be here! I only feel safe when Uncle Eddy is here.

He's going to be in Africa for another whole fortnight. But I know that he is thinking of me. He told me before he went. He said, "Sweetheart, when I'm away from you never a day goes by but you're in my thoughts."

I am going to concentrate on being in Uncle Eddy's thoughts. That way it will keep me safe.

Here is another joke I have thought of.

What did the dentist say in court?

I swear to tell the tooth, the whole tooth, and nothing but the tooth.

I suppose that is quite funny.

Sort of.

I can't think of any more.

It is no use asking Mum. She is like me, she can never remember the ending.

The ending of a joke is called "the punch line". It is a catastrophe if you cannot remember your punch line.

You would think that Mum would be able to, being an actress. But she has always had trouble with her lines. I have always had to help her.

I don't know who would help her if I was not here. She would have to manage on her own.

Danny is too young. He wouldn't be any good.

So nothing must happen to me or Mum won't ever be able to learn her lines!

Sarah told me a joke once. Something about seaweed.

Why is the sea wet? – Because the seaweed.

I think that was how it went. I can't really remember.

It was something like that.

Perhaps I am not a very jokey kind of person. Just a weedy wimpy sort of person who isn't very brave.

15. Wonderland

*You'd only been out of hospital for a few months
when you were told that you had to go back
in again.*

Mum cried when Dr Stanhope said I had come out of remission. She tried not to show it, but I knew she'd been crying because her eyes were all red and swimmy. So I knew that he had told her something bad.

Mum said that I was a little bit anaemic, "Just a little bit", and that Dr Stanhope wanted me to go back into hospital for some more treatment. I said, "Why do I have to go back into hospital for it?" Mum said, "Well, it's easier for them to keep an eye on you if you are in hospital. But I'm sure it won't be for very long."

I knew she wasn't telling me the truth. I knew that I had stopped being in remission. I do think it would be better if they didn't try to protect you. We can always tell.

When Dr Stanhope came to see me, I said, "Will you have to give me more chemo?" and he said, "I'm sorry, Becky, but I'm afraid we will." I said, "Is that because I'm not in remission any more?" and he said, "Yes, but let's hope it's just a hiccup."

When he said that I hiccuped, because that is the sort of thing they like you to do. They like you to be bright and sparky and have a sense of humour.

Dr Stanhope was pleased when I hiccuped. He laughed and said, "That's the spirit!"

Another time I said to him that someone had told me if you came out of remission before five years, it meant you probably wouldn't ever be cured. I didn't say it meant you would probably die, because I am not brave enough.

Dr Stanhope said, "It doesn't necessarily mean that at all. But it does mean it's more difficult. It does mean that you have to be extra specially brave and put up with another lot of treatment."

Zoë had to put up with another lot of treatment. So did Bryony, in my story that I wrote. And she grew up and danced in *Swan Lake*!

I know that Mum doesn't expect me to grow up. Nobody expects me to. Not even Dr Stanhope.

I suppose I don't, really. Deep inside myself. I know that what Zoë told me is true because Zoë is the one person who always tells the truth.

If Zoë were here I could talk about it with her. I

can't talk about it with Mum, it upsets her too much. She tells me not to be morbid. She says, "Oh, Becky, darling! Don't be so morbid!"

I don't think it's being morbid. And I don't think it's being negative, either, which is another thing Mum accuses me of. She says, "You must think positively, sweetheart! Otherwise you're not giving yourself a chance."

I don't see that it's being negative to wonder what is in store for you. I think it is simply facing up to things.

I've been thinking just lately about what Gran said. Gran said that when you die you meet all the people that have gone before. But wouldn't this make it terribly crowded? In heaven, or wherever it is that you go?

I tried asking Uncle Eddy about it. He is the only person I can really talk to, now that Zoë is not here. I said, "If everyone that's died is going to be up there, won't it be a bit like Oxford Street at Christmastime?"

I went to Oxford Street last Christmas with Ana-Maria to see the lights.

There were so many people you could hardly move.

Uncle Eddy said, "It will only be like Oxford Street if that is how you would like it to be. Is that how you would like it to be?" I said, "No, it isn't! I'd hate it!

Everyone pushing and shoving."

So then Uncle Eddy said, "In that case, think how you would like it to be, and that is how it will be."

I have been thinking and thinking. All I can think of is that I want Gran and Kitty to be there.

And maybe some of the really great dancers that I have seen pictures of. Margot Fonteyn and Rudolf Nureyev and Anna Pavlova.

It would be brilliant if I could get to meet them! But mostly I just want Gran and Kitty.

I knew when Uncle Eddy came back from Africa specially to be with me that I was more ill than Mum let on. Poor Mum! She can't face up to it.

I can! I think.

Sometimes I can. Other times it just doesn't seem real, the thought of life going on without me.

Well, but it is not going to! Not yet. I am not ready to leave yet. I am going to go on *fighting*.

I was ever so pleased when Uncle Eddy came back. It was a truly golden moment when I saw him walking into the ward. I love him so much! And we have been able to have long, long talks like I can't do with Mum.

me and Uncle Eddy, talking

We chat for ages together! About all sorts of things. There's nothing I can't talk to Uncle Eddy about. Like for instance one time I asked him whether he really thinks there are lots and lots of people waiting for us when we die. If I'd tried asking Mum she'd have said, "Oh, darling! Don't be morbid. What's all this talk of dying?"

Uncle Eddy never tells me that I'm morbid. He understands that there are things I need to know. He said, "For sure! Lots and lots. No one will ever have to be lonely."

I said, "But do people wait? Do they wait for people?"

Like Granddad, for example. Granddad has been dead for a really long time. Longer than I have been alive. Suppose he got tired of waiting for Gran and found someone else?

Uncle Eddy said that he wouldn't have got tired. He said, "Time is different there. There is no time. Time stands still… for ever and ever. To Granddad it will have seemed like no more than a few seconds have passed."

So then I asked him something else that had been bothering me. Granddad was only fifty when he died, but Gran was quite old. How would Granddad have felt about his wife being an old person? How would Gran have felt about it? Would she mind him seeing her with grey hair and wrinkles while he was still young? Wouldn't it have upset them both?

Uncle Eddy said, "No way!" He said that things like age simply wouldn't matter any more. He said, "If it was Gran's dream to be young again, and to meet Granddad when he was young, then that is what she will have done."

He said, "We will all find whatever we want to find, and be just as we want to be. I promise you."

I said, "Are you absolutely sure?" Uncle Eddy said, "I'm absolutely positive."

So then I said, "But how can you *know*? How can anybody *know*?" and he said, "Trust me! I know."

I do trust Uncle Eddy. But I still can't help being anxious. I don't want to go there if I can't be with Gran and Kitty!

Another thing Gran said was that dying was worse for the people that are left behind than for the people it happens to. I suppose this is because of time in heaven standing still while time on earth just creeps. Like for Granddad it would only have seemed a few seconds while for Gran it was years and years.

Perhaps it is a sort of comfort to think that people who have died are not being lonely and missing you. If I die it will only be seconds before I see Mum and Danny and Uncle Eddy again.

But I am not going to die! I don't want to! I want to dance Odette and go to Wonderland!

It's Danny I feel sorriest for. He is the one I worry about. I know that Mum will be sad and cry but she is always so busy with her television work and Uncle Eddy has his filming but Danny is only just a little boy. He won't understand! He won't know about time seeming like seconds. He won't know that there are people up there waiting for you.

Danny is going to miss me more than anyone. He'll be all on his own with Ana-Maria. And if she goes back to Spain he will have to get used to someone else and he is so shy, he hates having to meet new people.

I think Mum ought to have another baby to keep him company. I wouldn't mind her having another one. But first she will have to get married again and I don't know who she could marry. She hasn't even got a man friend at the moment. But it isn't fair to leave Danny on his own! He needs someone to look after him.

I wish I'd been nicer to him when he was a tiny baby. I wish I hadn't been jealous, because of him having a dad and me not. It wasn't his fault. He didn't ask to be born. Nobody asks to be born. I wish I'd cuddled and kissed him more. I love him ever so much!

When we go to Wonderland, Danny is going to come with us. I'm not going to go if Danny can't come! We oughtn't to have left him behind that night when we went to celebrate. The night Mum bought champagne. He can't help it if he's a silly babyish nuisance and bangs on the table and tips his chair back and does all those things that make Mum mad.

"He'd only ruin it for you." That's what Mum said. But I wouldn't have minded!

When we go to Wonderland, we will go on Concorde.

Mum has said that we can! She says it will be a special treat, for being twelve.

I shall be twelve in… a few months.

Three months!

Less than three months.

Soon.

Then we'll pack up our cases and Mum will say, "Have you put your toothbrush  in?" And Danny will want to take his teddy bear and Mum will groan and say, "Can't we go *anywhere* without that wretched bear?" But it's the only way that Danny will sleep.

He has nightmares if he's parted from Teddy.

Danny will take Teddy and I will take my signed photograph of Darcey. I don't go anywhere without my signed photograph. I've had it on my locker all the time I've been in hospital. The nurses call me their little dancer. They all know I'm going to dance in *Swan Lake*. Once when it was Carol's birthday they had a party for her on the ward and I did a snowflake dance that I made up myself, specially for her.

I danced it in my nightie! It was the nearest I could get to a proper ballet dress.

I made it about snowflakes because outside it was cold and snowy and people's mums and dads kept saying things like, "My goodness, you're in the best place in here!" It made Zoë ever so mad. She said, "How would they like it if they had to be in here?"

Zoë's at home now. She's doing really well. She sent me a card the other day.

I have good feelings about Zoë: she is going to be all right.

POST CARD

Hi Becky,
I'm well, why aren't you?
What are you doing in hospital??? Get back into remission!!! Quickly!!!
That is an order.
I MEAN IT.
ZOE xxxxxxxxx
xxxx Your Friend xxx
xxxxxxxxx
xxxx
P.S. Do it soon, OR ELSE!

Beck
Bar
Tu
IN

I still wish she could come to Wonderland with us!
It is going to be the very best birthday present I have
ever had. Uncle Eddy will come and pick us up in his car

and we will all drive to the airport together.

Then we will get on the plane

and do up our seat belts

and fly high up into the air

all across the seas and the oceans and the mountains

high amongst the clouds

and all through the stars

until we come to Wonderland!

All our favourite characters will be there.

There will be Jo, and Alice, and Peter Pan, and Lassie, and the Little Princess, and Dorothy – and Toto!

And my gran! My gran will be there! She'll be there, waiting for me!

I can't wait to be twelve and go to Wonderland!

That is the end of Becky's story.

She would have been so proud if she could see her name in print!

Who knows? Maybe she can…

In memory of our brave
little Becky Bananas
aged 11 years and
10 months
Be happy sweetheart
We love you
Mum, DANNY
and Uncle Eddy
'She had lots of bottle'

Fruit and Nutcase

"Hi, this is Mandy Small telling her life story."

I may have trouble writing, but I have no trouble at all talking!
My teacher, Cat, suggested I record my life on tape so
here goes...

I live with my dad, who looks like Elvis, and my mum, whose
idea of a special meal is burnt toast. Sometimes I feel like I'm
the grownup and they're the kids.

But now everything's crashing about my ears, and Dad's too,
as he's just put his foot through the floorboards. I'm trying
really hard not to become a total fruit and nutcase...

0 00 712153 9

Skinny Melon

and me

This is the diary of me, Cherry Louise Waterton,
and I am writing for posterity, in other words
the future.

And do I have a lot to write! Mum's just re-married, but how
could she marry a man called Roland Butter – what kind of a
name is that? He's a total dweeb who sends me coded
messages and calls me Cherry pie. Yuck!

I've got my best friend, Skinny Melon, to cheer me up but I'm
not sure if even she can save me from Roland and his
messages, or work out what Mum's big secret is…

0 00 712152 0

The Secret Life of Sally Tomato

A is for armpit,
Which smells when you're hot,
Specially great hairy ones,
They smell A LOT.

Hi! Salvatore d'Amato here – call me Sal if you must – and I am not writing a diary! I'm writing the best alphabet ever. An alphabet of Dire and Disgusting Ditties.

I'm up to two letters a week, and I reckon it will take me the rest of term to complete my masterpiece. By then I plan to have achieved my Number One aim in life – to find a girlfriend. After all, I'm already twelve, so I can't afford to wait much longer...

0 00 675150 4

Boys on the Brain

"What are you doing?" I said.

"I am trying," panted Mum,
"to – get- out – of – these – jeans!"

Hi there. I'm Cresta and that's my mum – thirty-three going
on eighteen. Me and my friend Charlie have great plans: finish
school, get the grades and conquer the world! We've taken a
vow – No Boys before uni, but it's not easy with the gorgeous
Carlito and Alistair around… And how on *earth* can I put up
with a mother who has boys on the brain?

0 00 711373 0

www.**fire**and**water**.com
Visit the booklover's website

Order Form

To order direct from the publishers, just make a list of the titles you want and fill in the form below:

Name ....

Address ....

....

....

Send to: Dept 6, HarperCollins Publishers Ltd, Westerhill Road, Bishopbriggs, Glasgow G64 2QT.

Please enclose a cheque or postal order to the value of the cover price, plus:

UK & BFPO: Add £1.00 for the first book, and 25p per copy for each additional book ordered.

Overseas and Eire: Add £2.95 service charge. Books will be sent by surface mail but quotes for airmail despatch will be given on request.

A 24-hour telephone ordering service is available to holders of Visa, MasterCard, Amex or Switch cards on 0141- 772 2281.

Collins
An *Imprint* of HarperCollins*Publishers*